WHEEL
MOUNTAIN

C000023097

THE
WESSEX
WAY

Tim Woodcock

future
BOOKS

Dedication

For Luke and Kay

Author's Acknowledgements

For their help in compiling the route and their invaluable advices: The Rights of Way folk in Somerset, Wiltshire and Hampshire; Steve Padfield, Mendip CC; Steve Planck, The Mounties CC; Alistair McClean, USE. For back up, advice and technical support: Ralph Coleman Cycles, Taunton, Somerset. Tel: 0823 275822. For clothing and carrying kit: Agu (T W Rutter), Polaris, North Wave MTB shoes and Karrimor. Finally for supplying hardware: Timax MTB frames, Shocktech suspension forks, Madison (Shimano and Halson suspension forks), Michelin tyres, Dia Compe (NTi), USE.

First published in 1995 by

Future Books

a division of Future Publishing Limited
Beauford Court, 30 Monmouth Street, Bath BA1 2BW

Typeset and designed by D & N Publishing, Ramsbury, Wiltshire

Edited by John France

ISBN: 1 85981 060 8

Printed and bound by BPC Paulton Books Ltd.
A member of the British Printing Company

2 4 6 8 10 9 7 5 3 1

If you would like more information on our other cycling titles please write to:
The Publisher, Future Books at the above address.

CONTENTS

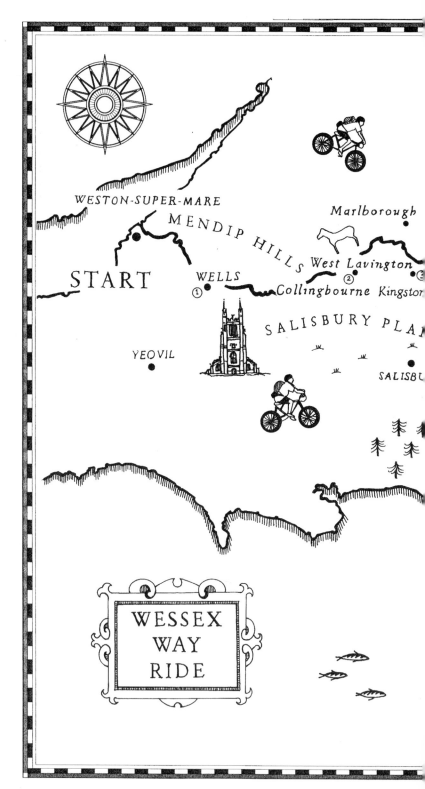

WESTON-SUPER-MARE

MENDIP HILLS

Marlborough

West Lavington

START

WELLS
①

② Collingbourne Kingston

③

SALISBURY PLAIN

YEOVIL

SALISBU

WESSEX
WAY
RIDE

SUGGESTED OVERNIGHT STOPS

① WELLS (30)
② WEST LAVINGTON (70)
③ COLLINGBOURNE KINGSTON (100)
④ DEANE (133)
⑤ BURITON (170)
⑥ UPPER BEEDING (205)
⑦ ALFRISTON (235)

④ Deane

WINCHESTER

⑤ Buriton

SOUTH DOWNS BRIGHTON

⑥ Upper Beeding

⑦ Alfriston

BEACHY HEAD

FINISH

INTRODUCTION

The Ride

The Wessex Way is a ride of epic proportions. The longest off-road, coast-to-coast ride in Britain. It takes a week to complete, traverses the breadth of the ancient kingdom to which it is dedicated and captures the essence that is off-roading in England's green and pleasant land.

Following ancient cart tracks and the oldest ridge roads in Europe the Way takes the upland route from Weston in the west to Eastbourne in the east, from one channel coast to another. Riding ridges of limestone and chalk, through the rolling hills of southern England, imparts such a sense of space as you soar, not cycle, from coast to coast. It's an astonishing experience, quite unexpected in a land so populated.

Built from debris deposited in warm seas millenia past, Wessex is a land of surprising contrasts. Mendip's wind-blown heather moors above Weston, the flat expanse of Somerset's fenland floor at your feet and the poppy-studded grasslands of Salisbury Plain. From the Plains the Wessex Way dips across the green and verdant finger of pasture land that is Pewsey Vale then trips along the edge of the Marlborough Downs. Here the mapped landscape's awash with gothic script and mysterious mounds that are the enigmatic remnants of our predecessors' tenure. On past Inkpen, high on an escarpment edge washed by golden fields of wheat and written into English literature in the words of *Watership Down*, where the Way swings south across the Hampshire Hills to climb the South Downs. A roller-coaster ride of subtle changes on quick, white tracks high above shimmering sea and forested farmscape. The end is abrupt. The sense of achievement immense.

The Rider

This may be one of the longest off-road rides in England but it's also one of the easiest. No need for you to be an ex-BMX whizz-kid. No trials' skills needed. You don't even need to be seriously fit – though being fit helps and pushes back the insidious effects of fatigue. No great map-reading skills are needed. Even the navigationally challenged, the

Much of the ride is over rolling downland like here near Houghton, West Sussex; but watch out for those sharp flints.

uninitiated off-roader or the born-again cyclist can set off from Weston and expect to complete the Way without fear or hesitation.

The Route

250 miles at a steady 700ft across southern England, over sumptuous, undulating landscapes make this ride a uniquely scenic experience. Summer-blue skies punctuated by curious cloud forms, white dusty tracks, dazzling to the eye, cut a swathe through rolling cornfields of feathered gold and disappear into the heat shimmer. A summer idyll that's hard to beat. Even after harvest, on winter days when frost freezes the land and the plough has turned gold to dun, riding ancient trackways across these rolling hills is full of rich rewards. And for those who like a technical edge to up the adrenaline factor winter wet can turn the chalk tracks of the South Downs into linear ice rinks and Mendip limestone is slicker than Slick Rock. Taken in downhill mode with a load on the bike it all goes ballistic before you can shout 'wipe-out!'

A coast-to-coast ride across the southern counties could easily be an endless slog in a bog but the Wessex Way follows in footsteps that have trodden the drier, higher ridge routes from pre-history. But 'drier' is a relative term and, except in high summer and in a real winter freeze, some sections will be gloopy. After a dry spell the entire route can be ridden in four or five days but any hint of wet and we're talking a full week – or more. Early summer is the ideal time to make the journey – rainfall and undergrowth is low – and going east will normally put prevailing winds at your back. Wind direction is a key factor – rolling hilltops are exposed!

From Inkpen Beacon eastwards the Wessex Way shares much of its route with two, well-established walks: The Wayfarer's Walk and The South Downs Way. Please take special care on these sections as you are most likely to meet walkers and horses.

Day Rides

If you are unable to make a week of it, the Wessex Way can easily be split into day rides. The route mainly follows escarpment edges and is ideally suited for sectioning into there-and-back rides, where the return trip gives a different and often unexpected perspective. I've also included three day-loop rides (see pages 89–94) to titillate the skills of the more experienced rider. Each connects with the Wessex Way so they can be added on for those who have a fortnight to spare!

BEFORE YOU GO

The Wessex Way is primarily a ridge ride and, as a broad generalisation, once you're up you're up. Even the highest summit – Beacon Batch at just over 1000ft – is dispatched on the first day so much of the route is pretty easy-going in mountain bike terms. That's until you get to the last few days. The seaward end of the The South Downs don't hang back when it comes to hill climbs so be prepared for some 600ft calf-grinders stacked end to end!

As long-distance rides go this one welcomes newcomers to the sport, not the physically challenged but you don't have to be an athlete either. Being in excellent shape to take a mountain bike across the chalk uplands of Wessex is an ideal but not altogether necessary. Providing you have time to tackle the first half in small stages you can gain fitness on the trail. The key is to give your body sufficient time to recover – especially if the old limbs get a bit lack-lustre and go stiff – and to slot in regular rest days. If, like me, you don't have all the time in the world to ride the Wessex Way then think about getting trim some weeks before the departure date.

I know it puts paid to travelling on a whim and the word 'preparation' rears its ugly head but being that bit fitter will make the whole escapade a great deal more fun for everyone. Even experienced MTBers who get out and hit the hills on a regular basis will benefit from some serious working out on their wheels. By the time you get to Weston thirty or forty miles off-road riding ought not to be an awesome ordeal.

Rides like this are an enriched experience if you're in good company. But travelling companions are notoriously tricky to choose and in the ups and downs betwixt the beginning and the end there will be stresses and strains. Long distance off-roading is not all fun. Even on England's green and pleasant hills a 600ft climb can be both difficult and demanding; add fatigue, perhaps a misread map and a ferocious wind and you've got a pretty good recipe for a falling out. Always distressing, discord can soon develop into dispute and that could be dangerous in the wrong place at the wrong time. Choose companions carefully.

Kitting Out

HARDWARE

'Weight is wearisome'. Whatever you've got you've got to carry it on this trip. Experienced off-roaders may be lulled into thinking that the undulating nature of this lowland landscape should allow some extra kit to be carried. Don't be fooled! Most of the climbs may be short but they're sharp. Trimming kit to a necessary minimum makes sense. Providing you don't overdo it and skimp on essentials, saving weight is safer too. It conserves energy and makes handling the bike on some of the steeper descents a lot less hairy.

The Wheels

Bike choice is a personal thing, fads and fashions change on a whim and depend more on who's racing what than what makes a fine MTB. Providing it's sound, any clunker of an MTB will do. Even a good quality trail or hybrid bike could be used. Having said that there are some pointers as to what makes a bike well suited to the task and what does not.

You're going to travel some steep and traction-testing trails so use a good quality, reasonably light, proper MTB – 21 or more indexed gears – with alloy wheels, low gearing and a comfortable saddle. Take a look at the mountain biking press for what's what or ask at a good mountain bike shop. It is essential that your bike is thoroughly serviced and checked out before setting off.

Some bike accessories that should be considered essential are: bottle cages – or piggy-back drink carriers if you're not using a rucksack, a brand new set of the best brake blocks you can afford and some branded, good quality treads, with around a 2in carcass of new rubber. Consult a good MTB bike shop for what's the latest trend in tyres and avoid cheap 'imitations'.

Other items to consider, especially if long-distance off-roading really grabs you, are: an A headset or a headset lock-ring, Allen-key crank fittings, a bomb-proof set of wheels, puncture-proof tubes and some sort of suspension, true or otherwise, to fend off fatigue. Pedal clips are essential when cycling off-road. Newcomers to the,sport are quite understandably nervous of clipping themselves to 25lbs of speeding steel tubes but in the end it's safer and more energy efficient.

The South Downs Way can become a bog in winter, so good clothing is essential.

Pannier racks and long-distance off-roading can be a mis-match. They simply disintegrate under the strain of bouncing over miles of boulders. Thankfully the Wessex Way sticks pretty much to well-worn tracks and a pannier rack can take the load, give your back a rest and act as a mudguard. Do buy a top quality rack and preferably a hollow-tubed, chrome alloy one. An alloy rack will crack sooner or later. Lastly, rack bolts come loose, so put a touch of Loctite on them when you fit the rack.

Tools and Spares

Quality tools are a godsend when you're in a fix. Most multi-tools will save weight, but don't forget to check that your clever widget does all the whatsits on your bike. And your partners'. The same goes for spares. If you all run the same tyre valves, chains, straddle wires and even brake blocks the stores can be kept to a sensible size. Once you've got all tools and spares together pack them tight and keep them handy. Don't expect a bike shop when you need one. There won't be one! You'll have to drop off the ridge you're riding and then it may be another 20 miles away!

SOFTWARE

Given that early summer is the ideal time to go versatility is going to be the vital ingredient, changeable weather the name of the game. If there's a hint of air movement down in the vales then the crest of a chalk ridge is going to have a fresh breeze blowing over it. There's nothing more miserable than a cold, wet mountain biker clad in inadequate clothing, so a key element in your wardrobe selection is going to be windproofing.

Dress Sense

Clothes designers are rising to the difficult challenge of meeting the needs of the mountain biker and there's a stack of really good, MTB-specific gear to choose from. The multi-layer principle works, but there are excellent single-layer systems as an alternative. However, this bonded pile/Pertex kit is really late season/winter wear, ideal for weight-saving freaks and fanatics who take to the mountains off-season.

So right from the start we're faced with a bewildering choice of kit. The best approach is to decide what you want the clothing to do. For long trips it has to be light, have low bulk, be quick-drying, resist the rampant sock syndrome, be easy to care for, fit well, feel comfortable and perform well. Whether it's to wick, provide warmth, windproofing or water resistance, you'll need clothing to perform all of these functions. Above all it must let your body 'breath'. Under-layer clothing that soaks up water and dims the lights when the tumble drier's turned on are useless. Likewise a top-layer that's built like a tent and gives you your very own greenhouse effect is best left at home and used as a bin-liner.

Comfort après-trail is fundamental to your well-being. You'll want to have a shower and step into some light clothes. Pack-down bulk and weight is especially important with après-trail togs.

On your feet there's nothing to beat a good pair of MTB boots but there are other options. Light walking boots and even fell-running shoes, with modified soles, are good alternatives. Both grip well, give ankle support and walking boots are great for keeping your feet dry. Most walking (a euphemism for pushing the bike!) will be on grass or mud and MTB boots with big grips on would be a real bonus. Don't be tempted by making do with trainers unless you're good at grass skiing with a bike on your back. Last, but definitely not least, wear a helmet!

Navigation Aids

Dispense with the bulky package of maps that's the bane of most long-distance rides. They're in this book. Add to that a good quality compass on a neck cord and a weather-proof cycle computer – both of which you must be able to use with ease – and that's the pilot part sorted.

Health and Survival Gear

Mountain biking can be dangerous; this ride may not be technically demanding but some descents are steep and potentially dangerous. A good first-aid kit and the knowledge to use it are essential. A basic kit should include antiseptic wipes, plasters, cohesive tape for wounds, triangular bandage, salt tablets for cramp, puritabs and first-aid instructions (see page 22). Survival gear – mini-torch, survival bag and whistle – can all be packed with the first-aid kit. Pack it in a heavy-duty, zip-tie polythene bag, label it clearly and know where it is. Not strictly first aid but pretty important are medicaments for treating minor ailments like saddle soreness (more common than you might imagine, but Sudacream or E45 cream soon speeds recovery), athlete's foot, sunburn, lip chaff, muscle strain and pain.

Other Stuff

Mountain biking's a dirty business so the personal hygiene department needs careful thought. Apart from the usual salves and unguents for bodily application some micro-wash liquid is a good idea to keep those shorts clean and fresh on a day-to-day basis. It helps prevent saddle sores too. Remember also that you'll need a small, quick-drying towel.

In the Bag

Backpack or pannier bag – which should you use? Opinions differ, and the truth is that it all depends on the terrain and for the Wessex Way let the bike take the strain. There's little in the way of radical rock and rubble to upset the balance of the bike, so the extra weight on the frame shouldn't be a problem. I would suggest you avoid twin panniers unless they're very small. They encourage you to overload. Best by far is the top-mounted pannier bag. There are even a couple of MTB-specific ones of about 30l capacity that can be swopped from rucksack to a pannier rack and back with ease. Together with either a bum bag or a small bar bag you should have quite enough luggage space.

If you're a rucksack freak then keep it to about 30l capacity. Features to look for are a narrow profile, light weight, waist security strap, wide shoulder straps (easily adjusted and locked, compression straps) and low pack height. Try it out, packed full, with your helmet on.

If you have problems packing all your kit, then try rolling the clothes into tight cylinders, holding them down and tying them with compression straps (velcro straps are ideal). Remember to put the least dense gear at the bottom, the heaviest at the top and ensure the back-panel is comfortable against your spine.

Wessex Way Kit List

A handy, 'pre-flight' check list is provided but don't regard it as definitive. Lists are an important aid to successful trip planning – a finely honed trip list is invaluable – and making your own will encourage you to evaluate each item on its merits. Try the one below for starters.

If you're expecting cold, wet weather you'll need to add extra clothing, especially thermals, tights, tops, windproof trousers, socks, full gloves, headband/snood and waterproof socks. In winter an extra-warm fleece/windproof top, for if you're caught in the open, lined mitts and lined hood may be necessary. On the hardware side don't forget lights.

How heavy will this lot weigh? For a summer crossing aim for about 14lbs for all your personal kit and about 7lbs of shared gear (including food). With three up you'll each have about 16lbs of kit on board.

TOOL KIT
Pump
Tyre levers
Full set of Allen keys
Small, adjustable wrench
Screwdriver (cross-head
　and flat)
Chain-splitter
Spoke key
Penknife

BIKE SPARES
Inner tube
Puncture repair kit
Brake blocks
Straddle wire
Lube
Rear gear cable
Rear light/batteries
Cable ties
Allen bolts for bottle
　cages etc
Gaffer/carpet tape
Couple of spare chain
　links
Cable lock
Water bottle(s)

CYCLE CLOTHING
Padded shorts
　(2 pairs min.)
Sports socks
　(3 pairs min.)
Cool shirt, short-sleeved
Cycle shirt, long-sleeved
Wicking/thermal top
Bike mitts
Helmet (not the
　elongated, aero-type)
Fleece/mid-layer top
Windproof top with
　hood
Waterproof top
Tights (great for keeping
　mud off your limbs)
MTB Boots

APRÈS TRAIL
Light-weight longs
Underwear
Shorts
Baseball boots/sandals or
　similar

PERSONAL KIT
Wash kit inc. towel
Zipped wallet with
　money
Plastic
YHA card/B&B contacts
Pencil
Sewing kit (polyester
　thread)
Medical kit
Head torch/batteries

TRAIL KIT
Compass
Computer
First-aid kit
Survival kit
　(whistle, bag, torch)
Emergency food
　(cereal bars etc.)
Rucsac with liner
Bar/bum bag (to keep em-
　ergency kit separated)

A few last strains of the calf muscles across Fyfield Down in Wiltshire, before a well-earned rest.

Accommodation

From the first one of the key considerations is where you are going to sleep. Even how you are going to sleep. Comfort and and a good night's rest are keynotes to the success of long-distance cycling and only you will know what your absolute needs are. Consider them carefully – you owe it to yourself.

Camping

Camping and self-sufficiency seem to go hand-in-hand with the adventure of mountain biking but – and it's a big but – the penalties are high. For a start there are no camp sites right on the route so you'll be relying on kind farmers to find you a dung-free field. Then the tent, stove, sleeping bag, mat, cooking kit and food plus additional clothes and the out-sized rucksack to put it all in will weigh you down by an extra stone or so and reduce your hill climbing ability to a slow crawl or push. Descents are interesting though, if lethal! Survivors, exhausted by a day beneath their burden, will then have the pleasure of finding a pitch, setting up the tent, searching out a water supply (there are no streams on chalk downland), fetching the water and washing cold. Then it's cook, eat, clean up and finally fall into a stupor only to be driven spare at the crack of dawn by a demented bunch of birds doing their dawn chorus thing! Camping's great.

Bed and Breakfast

By way of comparison, at the opposite extreme, we have B & Bs. First and foremost you can dump all that bulky camping kit and ride light. Not day-ride light but nimble enough to loft wheels, bunny hop and skip the rear end over the odd rut. And that's handy. It's a lot of fun too! Add to that an end-of-day cuppa followed by a deep, hot bath, supper in the pub, uninterrupted sleep, a breakfast to build a day's trail blazing on and the pleasure of being the guests of some of the best hosts one could wish for and you've got real luxury. But it costs and, in season, pre-booking is advisable. That means some sort of timetable. That said B & Bs are the best bet, most are well-used to catering for muddy Ridgeway walkers and there are plenty to choose from if you're happy to drop off the hills.

Youth Hostels

Somewhere between the two alternatives are Youth Hostels. You need only carry the same kit as for B & Bs and they're much cheaper. Most provide a full range of services from shop to showers and if you're not the self-catering type breakfast and evening meal can be a convenient opt-out. Add to that the best YHA idea – the drying room – and you can see hostels are handy. On the downside mucking in with a bunch of strangers night after night isn't always ideal, accommodation is in single-sex dormitories and sharing a hostel with a bunch of hyper-active juveniles still trying to fight their way free of the education system is not fun!

YHAs are few and far between along the Wessex Way until you get to the South Downs. Then there's one every few miles! All of them are listed separately (see page 95). Pre-booking is prudent in high-season and be warned; those jolly school parties are a maverick in the accommodation calendar at any time. Many hostels, like B & Bs, have a closed season so the accommodation logistics of a winter crossing need more careful planning.

ON THE RIDE

Getting There

In a perfect world we'd be able to grab our bikes, catch a train to
Weston, off-road it to Eastbourne and jump on a train home. But
British Rail is not very biker-friendly so you may find that this is so
inconvenient, when BR's restrictions and regulations are taken into
account, it is simply not practical. The key rule is to check, recheck
and book everything in advance. At this time it is possible to train it
from Eastbourne, via Gatwick and Reading, back to Weston with up to
five bikes subject to space. So you could drive to Weston and take it
from there.

Road access to Weston is excellent – the Wessex Way begins just 5
miles from junction 21 on the M5. Only those coming up from the
Dorset/Hampshire coast would use a different route and for them it's
the A36 to Bath then the A39/A368 route, in the lee of the Mendips,
to Weston.

Off-road Biking

Ride safe. Ride light. Being the new boys on the block, mountain
bikers have run the gauntlet of being alienated by other countryside
users from the word go. The sport has mushroomed and our wilderness
areas have witnessed a wheeled invasion feared by some other
countryside users.

The fact that it's a rerun of early rambler-versus-landowner conflicts
makes no difference. Neither does the fact that the hoary chestnuts of
'tyres tear up trails' and 'bikers are the beasts of the bridleways' are
perceived, not proven, concerns of some of our countryside
companions. In fact recent, carefully-controlled studies have conclu-
sively shown that a good off-road cyclist causes no more trail damage
than a walker. So we're here to stay and entrenched attitudes are already
changing. This will come about more quickly if we ride responsibly.

Rights of Way

Although we've taken every care to try and ensure that the mapped
Wessex Way and Day-Ride routes will keep your cycling within the

law, the status of some sections is likely to change. Plus, it is possible you may get lost so it is as well to be sure of your rights of way.

Off-road cycling is permitted on bridleways, roads used as public paths (RUPPs), byways open to all traffic (BOATs), unclassified county roads (Greenways) and designated cycle paths. Some of the Forestry Commission roads are open to us with the landowner's consent but this permissive access may be revoked at any time. Cycling is not permitted on footpaths, open land or on pavements. Do not rely on signposts as reliable indicators of a route's status. If in doubt dismount. And remember, all land is owned by someone and you must take care not to trespass. If a landowner asks that you leave it is in your best interests to acquiesce.

Of course you may be bowling along a bridleway when you find the way barred. It's a tricky situation because your rights say you can remove the obstacle sufficiently to get past if it is reasonably possible or make a short detour to get round it. The landowner can demand recompense if you cause any damage so be careful. If a way is blocked, farmers are supposed to provide signed, alternative routes, but if you're in doubt don't traipse across regardless. Check with the owner and if you're still forced off the Right of Way report it to the local authority (addresses are given on page 96).

Codes of Conduct

In following the Wessex Way off-road route you will be riding in the tyre tracks of others, and others will follow you, so behave responsibly and follow the Country and Off-road codes. This will help ensure all will receive a warm welcome from the countryside community.

Ride Safety

Three's company, not two, and four's fine outdoors. In the event of one getting badly injured someone can go for help and someone can stay with the casualty. But ideally two should go for help, which is why four is better. Any more and mountain bikers can be an intimidating party.

Abilities, strength and stamina vary. Keep within the capacity of everyone, watch your pace and make sure everyone keeps within sight of each other. But don't bunch up, especially on downhills, or there'll be some rear-end wipe-outs. It's always a good idea to wait for

Breezing through a leafy tunnel on the way up to Fyfield Down, near Pewsey, Wiltshire.

stragglers at the top of climbs, at the bottom of tricky descents and at gates. One of the first signs of fatigue is when your normally ebullient companion rides quietly and persistently lags behind. Don't push it. Rest, drink, eat and keep warm – exposure may be just around the corner. Prevention is better than cure. Eat well at supper and breakfast. Don't be over-confident when assessing how far you can travel during the day and allow a generous amount of extra time if the going gets muddy. Don't ride for more than an hour without some food, and drink regularly before you get thirsty. Always wear enough to keep warm and, if you stop in cold weather, put an extra layer on.

Weather

Out on the Downs weather will make or break a day. Except on a winter's crossing cold is unlikely to be a big problem but get wet and the wind-chill can rob a body of warmth at an alarming rate. Add injury to the equation and things can get serious so get the most recent weather forecast – telephone numbers are given on page 95 – and make a habit of catching the TV weather forecasts each evening.

Three factors that newcomers to off-road cycling often fail to take into account are altitude, wind and winter. As you climb temperature falls. Okay so the Wessex Way climbs no mountains but for much of the time it's 500 or 600ft above the surrounding countryside. And, as the following figures show, that extra height can add a nip. Roughly speaking temperature falls 1°C for every 100m gain in height (3°C per 1000ft) on a clear day, half that fall on a cloudy one. Wind-chill increases with wind strength. In a gentle to moderate breeze (force 3, about 10mph) wind-chill is about −5°C, about −10°C in a fresh, gusty breeze (force 5, about 20mph) and −15°C in a really strong wind (force 7, about 30mph). So if you're planning a winter crossing it's as well to bear in mind that temperatures will be 10–15°C colder than in summer. Nippy!

Losing Your Way

Navigation can be tricky. Keeping on course depends on you, and preferably your companions as well, knowing your position at ALL times. Danger zones are forests, open downland and in poor visibility so take care to read the terrain correctly in these situations and make no assumptions about this or that trail being a 'main' route. One way of coping with poor visibility is to follow a compass bearing to the most distant visible marker (not a sheep because it might walk off!), cycle to it, take another bearing on the next marker, cycle and so on.

You'll be riding on obvious tracks and paths for 99% of the time so you are more likely to feel lost than really be lost. But there's always an outside chance you might wander from the route. Don't panic. Stop. Make sure everybody's with you and then try to work out where you went wrong. Not too far back you'll have been sure of your position. Find it on the map. Having used your cycle computer to keep a log of point-to-point distances, it's a simple matter of reading the distance off and calculating direction to give you an approximate position. Forgotten to zero the trip distance at the last known point? Then estimate how far you've cycled. Now check your surroundings and see if local landmarks coincide with your findings. It goes without saying that correct use of the compass and trusting it, not your instincts, is vital.

Up on the Downs mists are a regular occurrence and in poor visibility it's possible to be unsure of your whereabouts. If this is the case then descend north and you will find a road within 4 or 5 miles. Cycle to a signpost and take it from there.

Accident Procedure

It's vital that at least one of the party is a qualified first-aider. Ideally all of you should know the fundamentals of first-aid. The British Red Cross, St John's Ambulance and St Andrew's Ambulance Societies all run courses so, if you haven't done so already, book into one. Carrying a proper first-aid kit with instructions and being a competent first aider is an essential part of accident procedure. But first-aid instructions don't always cover the common illness and injuries associated with mountain biking. These are given below:

Hypothermia

(exposure – the most common cause for rescue calls)

SYMPTOMS:

Complaints of fatigue; cold, visual abnormalities; lethargy, lack of interest; cold, clammy skin, pale in colour; slurred speech; cramps; clumsiness; odd behaviour; out-of-character actions; collapse and coma. Assume exposure if two or more of these symptoms are apparent and treat immediately.

ACTION:

Stop. Do not continue in the hope that you'll find shelter. **Shelter the patient.** Wrap them in extra clothing and put them in the survival bag, with someone else if possible. If you have a sleeping bag then use it as an inner layer. **Warm the patient** with bodily companionship and a warm drink if possible. Easily digested energy food can be given provided the patient is not too drowsy. **Cheer the patient up** – low moral is a contributory factor. Be positive – the rest of the group will be feeling pretty worried. **Rest the patient** for a prolonged period. If there's any doubt about the patient's ability to recover then send for help. **Look for signs of exposure** in other members of the party and signs of frostbite if conditions are severe. **Do not rub** the patient to restore circulation. **Do not give alcohol** – it may cause collapse.

In extreme cases, patients sometimes stop breathing so be prepared to give mouth-to-mouth, and if the patient does lose consciousness place them in the recovery position. **Seek Medical Help**

Frostbite

(long descents and winds in winter are common causes)
<u>SYMPTOMS:</u>
Prickling pain; numbness; skin may discolour blue or white; skin may feel hard.
<u>ACTION:</u>
Warm the affected area with additional body heat only. Extremities are the most commonly affected areas and can be placed in the armpit or crotch. The face can be covered with dry, gloved hands. **Remove rings**, watches, boots etc to ensure free blood flow. **Return to civilisation** and get the patient to hospital if at all possible or get help. **Do not rub** the affected area. **Do not apply heat** from an artificial source. **Do not use a revitalised limb** or the affected tissue will tear.

Heat Exhaustion

(common during periods of sustained effort)
<u>SYMPTOMS:</u>
Pale, sweaty skin; complaints of dizziness, fatigue and headache; cramps; rapid but weak pulse; shallow breathing; fainting.
<u>ACTION:</u>
Shade the patient. Find a cool, shady spot and lie them down. **Cold drinks of water**, slightly salted and with a little sugar if possible, will soon aid recovery. **Seek Medical Help**

Heatstroke

(severe heat exhaustion)
<u>SYMPTOMS:</u>
Restlessness; frequent passing of urine; complaints of dizziness and headache; hot, flushed, dry skin; rapid, strong pulse; fainting.
<u>ACTION:</u>
Cool the patient by placing them in shade and remove their clothing. **Sponge their body** with water until their body temperature drops and they appear to recover. **Seek Medical Help Immediately**

Shock

(present in almost all cases of traumatic accidents)
<u>SYMPTOMS:</u>
Pale and pallid skin, especially the lips; rapid, weak pulse; rapid, shallow breathing; cold, sweaty skin; complaints of dizziness and blurred vision; Restlessness; yawning, pronounced sighing; fainting.
<u>ACTION:</u>
Reassure the patient. External

A feature of Southern England in spring and early summer is the bright yellow fields of rape; what a smell too!

bleeding or other injuries should be treated simultaneously. **Lie the patient down**, but keep warm and avoid unnecessary movement. **Turn their head to one side. Raise their feet** on a pile of clothes or small rucsac. **Loosen restrictive clothing. Control Body Temperature** with loose clothing. **Do not give food or drink. Do not apply heat** from an artificial source. **Seek Medical Help Immediately**

Dislocation

(elbow, shoulder and knee joints are most at risk)
SYMPTOMS:
Deformity of the joint, especially when compared to the joint on the opposite side of the body; swelling around the joint; lack of mobility; severe pain associated with the joint.
ACTION:
Support the injured limb in a comfortable position.
Use the triangular bandage for arm/shoulder dislocations when the patient can sit or stand, rolled-up clothes for the leg. **Do not try** to manipulate the joint. **Do not move** the affected joint unnecessarily. **Seek Medical Help**

Broken Collar Bone

(Perhaps the most common MTB fracture)
SYMPTOMS:
Patient supports injured arm against the body; head inclined towards the injured shoulder; lack of mobility in the injured side; swelling at the front of injured shoulder.
ACTION:
Position arm of injured side with fingers up towards the opposite shoulder, palm flat against the body, so far as the patient will allow. Place soft padding between the upper arm and body. Support the arm using the triangular bandage for an elevation sling off the good shoulder that encloses the elbow, forearm and hand. **Secure the arm** against the body with a belt or strap that encircles the body. **Do not move the injured arm** if it is too painful, support against the body in situ. **Seek Medical Help**

TO RIDE TO A WHITE HORSE

Weston's garish Grand Pier was mirrored in the still, steel-grey waters of the Bristol Channel. The seafront was empty bar a few folk enjoying an early morning constitutional in the curious quiet that is a seaside town at dawn. As we posed for an album snap, our only audience a haughty herring gull, it was hard to believe we stood at the start of a 250 mile (402km) off-road trek. A rambling track, right across southern England's ridgeways to Beachy Head. Another coast, another channel.

But before we stood on the white cliffs of Beachy there were six delicious days of dirt tracks and downland descents to savour. Why wait? We took off. Young Luke, a teenage lad on his first long ride, was well pleased to be pumping pedals at last!

Off-road rubber hummed on tarmac but not for long. Our tyres' first taste of dirt track was on the dark, damp, tree-clad slopes of Worlebury Hill. An overnight deluge had transformed this tame piece of path into an ice rink with an incline. The water tower atop the hill served as a waymarker for a swing right down to town. A sweet 'n steep descent on more wet limestone that had us slip-sliding from side to side and spat us out onto the streets of Weston with a might too much speed.

Weston was waking, bleary-eyed commuters cocooned in their cars were facing up to another daily grind. Our only grind was of the granny-cog variety on our first haul up onto the Mendip Hills. Before long we'd crested Bleadon Hill, a lone buzzard circled aloft and I was filled with a sense of having broken free. Now our off-road venture was truly begun! It was time to kick cranks and savour some gravity-suck on the mile-long descent to Loxton. We sped off, gathering speed in fine style, when two dapper little dogs appeared out of nowhere, trotting up the track, oblivious to the two bikes bearing down on them! I hit the anchors, but to little effect, and with less than five yards to impact it dawned on me that these were not dogs but foxes! The impending doom dawned on them too! They quit the track in a flash and we missed them by a whisker!

Into Loxton, over the M5 and straight into the single-track climb round Crook Peak. It turned out to be the only push 'n carry of the trip but begs for a return run in the downhill direction. Definitely a touch technical! On the Mendip Ridge we treated ourselves to a pit stop with a magnificent panorama. But we hadn't conquered the ridge yet, the day was still young and we had a long road ahead. Bratton beyond Westbury was our goal and that was still some 50 miles (80km) away! We dipped into the woods below Wavering Down and hit more slick-rock limestone, on a rampant little run down to the A38 in Dolebury Bottom. Beware! We barely brought ourselves to a halt before we hit the highway!

The 850ft ascent to Beacon Batch, at over 1000ft the highest hill on the Way, began innocently enough. Feeling pretty pleased that the climb was proving less severe than we'd supposed we emerged onto the open moor to be faced by a hostile hillside. Steep, with steps fashioned by horse hooves, it was a killer climb with a good dose of front wheel lift to liven it up. A trig point at the summit made a convenient back prop while we perused the route covered so far. Way out west the promontory of Wolebury Hill stood above Weston. Even a day ride from there would have been a challenge! We turned east, putting our backs to the Bristol Channel.

A short bit of peat path – the only acid soil encountered on the ride – took us down to tarmac that whisked us into Wells. England's smallest city, most mediaeval and whose cathedral has the finest west front in Europe. The climb up by King's Castle had a kink and a kick in its tail but was well worth the effort to escape from the roaring juggernauts that blast along the A361. Once again we were atop the Mendip Ridge and we cruised east, top-cogging it all the way to Chantry where we cut through the lanes to Nunney. Late afternoon sun sent temperatures soaring so we rested on the greensward by the castle, a fairytale fortress in miniature, complete with moat.

Revived and buoyed up by the sun's late arrival we set off across Selwood – once England's last remaining natural forest fastness, now just a few scattered coppices – for Somerset's border. This was the only stream crossing of the trip. There's a footbridge but we had to fly through the only ford. One county crossed, four to go.

Longleat's leafy cart tracks were still tacky from the recent rains and even modest climbs tested traction but the descents were a delight

Overleaf: Going for it through spectacular, open scenery at Barnsfarm Hill, Washington, West Sussex.

especially the long run into Warminster. In town we caught the scent of fish and chips, and after a hearty feast we picked up the old Westbury road and headed for the hills happy in the knowledge that we had just one more climb to conquer.

Despite the fatigue it was disappointing to find the ascent tarmac, but we hit the dirt – or mud as it turned out – soon enough. With that the land had undergone a sea change. Suddenly it was Salisbury Plain: the white mud and mellow hills of a classic, dry valley, downland landscape cut across by chalk 'n flint cart tracks. In the evening sun white track turned gold and we were transported to MTB heaven. A fitting finale to our first day. By the time we got to Bratton and our B & B at Birchanger Farm we were ready to hit the sack and sleep the sleep of the just!

Pale Trails over Plain and Vale

It was late morning, with the sun already heading for high noon, when we finally hit the road. No matter, we'd covered a fair chunk of the route on the first day and our limbs demanded a less daunting day.

Back above Bratton, with a fine ridge to ride along, we kicked the cranks and blasted along the pale, dusty trails in summer sun with just a kiss of wind to cool the climbs. Up above the Lavingtons expansive views opened up, birdsong filled the air and the rude interruptions of tarmac gave out at last. On Urchfont Hill the Plain has the atmosphere of remote moorland; being untouched and allowed to lie fallow for the military to fling shells at. One good reason why the Wessex Way trips lightly round the edge of the ranges! A peculiar fluorescent pyramid, a range marker that can be seen for miles, proved to be a convenient waymarker for our route off the Plain and into the pastoral landscape of the Vale of Pewsey. The track dips down a set of nicely packed contours to give velocity a kick. I was really humming but then an unexpected chicane gave grip the slip and the front tyre took a thorn, flatted fast and robbed me of the rest of the run down to Chirton. Luke appeared looking disconsolate. Ricocheting off the chicane had wrenched his rack and snapped a bracket.

Fortunately Karrimor's Rack-Packs quickly convert to backpacks and, with a zip-tie to keep the rack from rattling, the puncture repaired and the pack on Luke's back we were on our way again. A quick fuel stop at Chirton's service station, some well-timed R & R languishing in the sun and off again to the hills above Pewsey. We were faced with an overgrown, hoof-holed bridle path followed by a 500ft climb up chalky cart track that reflected enough heat to put a blast furnace to shame. Where had those cool zephyrs disappeared to?

Once we'd gained all that height there was little else to do but lose it. Fast! This time on grass where forty-plus isn't hard to reach providing there's no mutton moseying around. Up again for a granny-cog grind on grass to reach the summit of Golden Ball Hill – the last few yards get seriously steep – where our burned-out bodies were once again caressed by cool breezes. Heaven! Below the verdant Vale, a chequer-board of pasture and corn, spread like a table to the distant hills of the Plain. Well rested and with a wind-kissed ridge to ride we set off in ebullient mood.

The Oare Hill to Martinsell leg was well overgrown – *Urtica dioica* (mega-stingers) all over the place and they 'urt! We made a sharp exit from the painful path, rode free from vegetable attack in the fields alongside and picked up the path where the undergrowth was less abundant. At Clench we dropped off the ridge on a radical road descent. Luke shot ahead, keen to catch a cool slipstream.

All too soon we were heading for the foot of Fyfield Down up a Tolkeinesque tree tunnel. We emerged to face the toughest climb of the day. It kicked off with a plethora of pathways, all potholed by plodding bovine beasties and profiled in a wheel-bouncing waveform. A setting sun saw us grinding up the head of a golden valley but we had little energy left to take in the spectacle. My mind was on the long, cold beer waiting in The Cleaver at Collingbourne Kingston. Even with that incentive it took us another two hours before we were slaking thirsts.

Downs to Dummer

We'd planned to get away by ten but it was twelve by the time Luke's rack was rebuilt, a wayward wheel was trued and yet another flat fixed. Maintaining a leisurely pace the previous day had allowed the legs some respite and today we were spared the usual calf-strained stiffness. We climbed out of Collingbourne on chalk cart track and dipped into a dark and damp Collingbourne Wood. Back out into the blazing sun and it was time to break out the sun-block and shades. Our route dropped us into the head of Hippenscombe Bottom – a mysterious, meandering valley with intertwining spurs in perfect proportion – on a track that is downhill all the way to the llama farm at the bottom.

Past the farm we hit a bumpy, single-lane climb up Haydown Hill. Keeping to the central ridge was the only way to avoid the long arms of dog rose angling for a rake along an unwary biker's arms. A shady spot in Oxenwood gave us an excuse to stop for a mid-morning break and run through the route to come. Most of it would be on ancient byways along an escarpment edge with kingly views of the Kennet valley.

We connected with the ridge ride at Rivar where we were confronted with an abrupt climb-out straight off the road. We weakened and pushed. Luke reckoned we'd let ourselves down and vowed to stay in the saddle for the rest of the Way. But he hadn't reckoned with the ruts. A moment later and he was pitched screaming into a bed of nettles!

Lunchtime saw us atop the impressive col that straddles Combe Gibbett. We were loath to leave. The views were stunning. Luke had hoped that our linking in with the popular Wayfarer's Walk would see an end to overgrown trackways, but no such luck. With annoying regularity we'd find ourselves running the gauntlet of single-track sandwiched between serried ranks of nettles. The trick though, was to turn up the speed and slip through with barely a scratch let alone a sting.

Up above Highclere, broad, chalk, estate tracks gave us respite from repeated vegetable attack. Finally we could turn up the speed and put a bit of mileage down. By now the sun had shed most of its heat and time was getting on. We cycled through a sea of chrome-yellow rape set hard against the backdrop of a ballistic blue sky. There was no doubt that this ride scored high on the scenic scale. Up on Ladle Hill it was tempting to take ten, but we had no time to tarry now. The prospect of riding the final few miles in the dark was looming large. Plus we had no water. And fate, in a fit of whimsy, had us climbing the famous shoulder of Watership Down just when we were in most need of something wet. We enjoyed our final descent of the day on the flinty track across Cannon Down and pedalled into Walkeridge farm parched and in desperate need of water.

With the hills behind us we were happy to wind down and settled into an evening saunter along a medley of tracks and lanes. We connected with our last track of the day alongside a trio of off-roaders out for an evening's dirt shredding with the dogs. Despite the fatigue our long-distance ethic gave us the edge and we overhauled them – much to Luke's delight – and allowed ourselves a self-satisfied spin to Oakdown Farm in Dummer and a well-deserved shower and rest.

The sky over Black Down in the Mendips is appropriate to the place.

Dummer to the Downs

Dummer's a pretty spot. A compact, thatched village of leafy lanes where time passes slowly, though the motorway's no more than a few hundred yards away. Forecasts had promised a heat wave and by mid-morning shade-seeking was vital. So, while the Way in Hampshire frequently flounders about in bog, at least it's tree-lined and shadowed. I'd expected it to be flat. Dull in fact. But downhills there are a few and, with the added benefits of a cooling slipstream, we savoured every one.

Wall-to-wall vegetation with a bad attitude forced a detour by lane to Brown Candover. We'd hoped for a shop but Candover's corner store had disappeared. On to Alresford. Abbotstone Wood is a popular picnic site where the track finished and we were treated to a fine piece of winding, woodland path with sufficient downhill pull to entice the wheels to spin and rustle up some off-road rhythm.

The river came as a surprise. They're a rarity on this ride and the cool, crystal clear waters that slipped beneath the bridge looked so inviting until Luke caught sight of some cattle using the stream as a loo! Robbed of a refreshing dip the heat really hit us on the next hill. But the sweaty struggle up was rewarded by a steep sweep down the valley on a cool cart track beneath the trees. Bliss! Alresford is an elegant old market town with a wide main street and all the mod cons for some serious R & R, including a handy cold water tap in the town's main garage. Restocked and refreshed we took refuge behind a tree on the edge of Alresford golf course, grabbed a bite to eat and worked up the courage to cycle across. Only one thing for it but to put our heads down and pedal slowly, real slow, and hope.

On the way to Warnford we made the only navigational error of the trip. In our defence a fallen tree and an overabundance of undergrowth had hidden the entrance to our turning and even when we realised our mistake it took a while to find a way through. At Warnford we were leaving the gentle gradients of the Hampshire hills behind. Ahead lay the South Downs and some serious height gain starting with the ascent of Old Winchester Hill. The views over the Meon Valley were magnif-icent and the contemplation of all those South Downs descents to come kept my mind off the grind. The map showed our track tripping lightly down tightly-stacked contours to Whitewool Farm, so off we set.

Still buzzing on our dose of downhill adrenaline we dug into the climb up to HMS Mercury. It's a slippery slope, with a winding water runnel to avoid. Luke – that boy always seemed to be leading the climbs – never gave up either. So, despite my screaming calf muscles, I plugged on behind and we both made the top well pleased with our effort. The dip I was dreading between here and Butser never materialised, we kept our height and even had enough surplus energy to ride up and take in the panorama from the top. It was a summer's evening idyll; quiet and serene. Minutes later we were screaming down the precipitous, fast-grass descent to the A3, the speedo slipping past 40mph on an all-out freewheel (not to be recommended unless there's not a soul about!). Thanks Butser for that brief burst of manic magic!

Through Queen Elizabeth Country Park and on up to the Downs. We spun cranks and cruised along white tracks with our lengthening shadows running out before us. Driven on by Luke's worse-case scenario – no supper – we arrived at our B & B exhausted and anxious. Happily our kind-hearted host rustled up the biggest bowl of Bolognese we'd ever seen. Evidently she knew about teenage appetites and carbo-loading!

Ridge Top Roller Coaster

Day five saw us up and away late as usual. Brighton YHA was our objective. Not only a long stretch but we had a fair few leg-busting climbs to conquer – especially at the end of the day! Add to that a searing sun that sucked sweat out of your body quicker than a Kleenex and we knew we had our work cut out.

Cool breezes brushed across the undulating landscape of the South Downs ridge, tempered the temperatures a notch and with navigation simplified to 'straight on at all junctions', we picked a rut apiece, relaxed and went into cruise mode. Nature wasn't content to leave us with a smoothly contoured chalk ridge to ride; aeons ago she froze the porous rock solid, threw down a deluge or two then had rivers rasp out the odd ravine. Millenia mellowed the chalk chasms, warmth turned tundra to savannah, streams sunk out of sight and the classic South Downs dip was born. Our first dip of the day was Cocking Down and down was the operative word.

There's nothing like a bit of adrenaline to put some pep into the pedals, we top-cogged along the back bone of the Downs ridge and the miles slid serenely under the tyres. Dry now, the deeply rutted road beyond Littleton Farm is obviously a slough of slurry in winter. We kicked up a dust storm, clicked in 26–28 and clawed our way up onto Sutton Down. It was a long, desiccating drag. Whiteways Roundabout has a kiosk, toilets and Houghton Forest, between here and there, has some prime time single-track to ride. Why wait?

Fully refuelled and raring to go we dropped down into the Arun valley on a brilliant bit of bridleway. Dust clouds billowed off the berms as we carved into a tight chicane, outside leg ramroding the pedal to counter sideways slip, spinning through for a superlative run. Then it was granny-cog slog for the 600ft climb back up to the top. And the last bit's seriously, seriously steep!

With the clock running against us, we selected a spinning gear and hummed. Then my rack broke. Nothing that a cable tie couldn't fix but I rather fancied carrying the pack on my back for a change. Riding a light bike again was a revelation.

The enthusiasm was short-lived. After a dash with death crossing the A24 the climb to Chanctonbury was a killer. We took ten at the top but from now on there was to be no long ridge ride to recover on. It was straight back down to ground zero on the banks of the River Adur, bar the odd bit of asphalt and a flat field or two, then straight up some calf-singeing single-track to Truleigh Hill.

A short ridge ride allowed the quivering quadriceps time to regain their composure and some well-timed single-track dropped us into Saddlescombe, kicked up the fun factor and set us up to conquer the last climb of the day. A mind-numbing granny-cog slog up a precipitous grass slope. I hung on to Luke's tail as he was determined not to dismount. We made the summit, spirits soared, bodies sagged and we sailed down to the tarmac sea that's the A24 and breezed into Brighton well-pleased but dead beat.

Last Blast to Beachy Head

Nigh on a week's worth of Hispanic-style heat wave had brought pressure and humidity to hot-house heights. The over-stressed weather system burst with a spectacular splashdown. But the record-breaking drencher did nothing to clear the air. Visibility was virtually nil and the air was heavy. Sultry, sweat and singlet weather – not ideal for cycling. Today we might be glad of our waterproofs!

At Highclere in Hampshire you'll find Grotto Copse Gatehouse, and time for a well-earned rest if you need one.

Back to Pyecombe to pick up where we left off but this time the ridge offered no vantage point to enjoy the vistas. Thick haze hid most everything with just a hint, here and there, of the spectacular panorama we were missing. We spun cranks, eastward bound, on a bridleway that was to deliver us to Beachy Head at the end of the day. The scent of achievement was in the air.

The South Downs hang a sharp right some way west of Lewes. A brief bit of R & R on the junction allowed us to take stock of the misty scene ahead. There were some mighty hills – for all the world like grey whales on the landscape – and the highest just had to be where we were heading! A sobering thought. For now we had a fantastic, 1.5 miles of mild-mannered gravity suck to savour.

South of the A27 we were back to humpback hills, shooting down to sea level then back up to 600ft for a radical, roller-coaster ride that should have treated us to an ever-changing series of ridge-top views. But whatever we missed due to mist we made up for on the descents. Dropping into Alfriston we courted disaster on a slick and rutted run down chalk track. In the village we hit a tourist hot spot. We guzzled and gawped then made off for the hills again.

Just as we were getting into wind-down mode the wooded hill above Jevington dropped us into a refreshing bit of rooted single-track tucked in between the trees. Essence of MTBing! Suddenly we were out by the church and back to road mode on the meander through the village. Ahead was the last big climb of the day, in fact of the Way! I love last climbs. At the top Eastbourne should have been spread out below but we couldn't see a thing! Now it was heads down and hum for the finish.

In vain we searched the foggy horizon for signs of the sea. It was frustrating to know we were so near yet there was no end in sight. It was almost autumnal. The air lay heavy with humidity. Warm, grey skies spat desultory spots of rain at us. We were caught in the silence before a storm. It was only a matter of time before it broke. All of a sudden it was a race against the rain. We rushed headlong down Long Down, putting a flock of rooks to flight as we sped by. Still no sign of the sea. Just the ethereal outline of an old lighthouse perched on top of the cliffs. Side by side we struggled up the last, grass slope and suddenly the land stopped. We stood, astounded at the giddy heights of the chalk cliffs. The Wessex Way ran right out into thin air. And there at last, an awe-inspiring drop below, was our sea!

ROUTE ABBREVIATIONS AND INSTRUCTIONS

The route is split into eight days of riding, but this is only a guideline. The highlighted villages and landmarks on the maps correspond to key points in the route directions. A brief description of the day's ride, including parts of the route to watch out for, is provided at the beginning of each day's ride. Overnight stops are suggested but again only as a guideline.

The instructions are brief and to the point to make them easy to follow while riding. If in any doubt, always refer to the map and check your compass to ensure you are heading in the right direction. Compass directions are given after each turning.

The following abbreviations have been used:

Turn L : Turn left
Turn R: Turn right
SO: Straight on

Bad weather routes have been given where necessary.

KEY

 Map Orientation

 Technical Information

 Overnight Stops

 Off-Road Code

 **Bad Weather Route**

NOTE TO THE MAP SECTION:

The maps used are based upon the Ordnance Survey 1:50000 series which have been reduced by 20%. Therefore, one mile is equivalent to one inch and one kilometre to 1.6 cm.

Kilometres: 1 km   2 km

Statute miles: 1 m   2 m

MAP I

Sand Fm

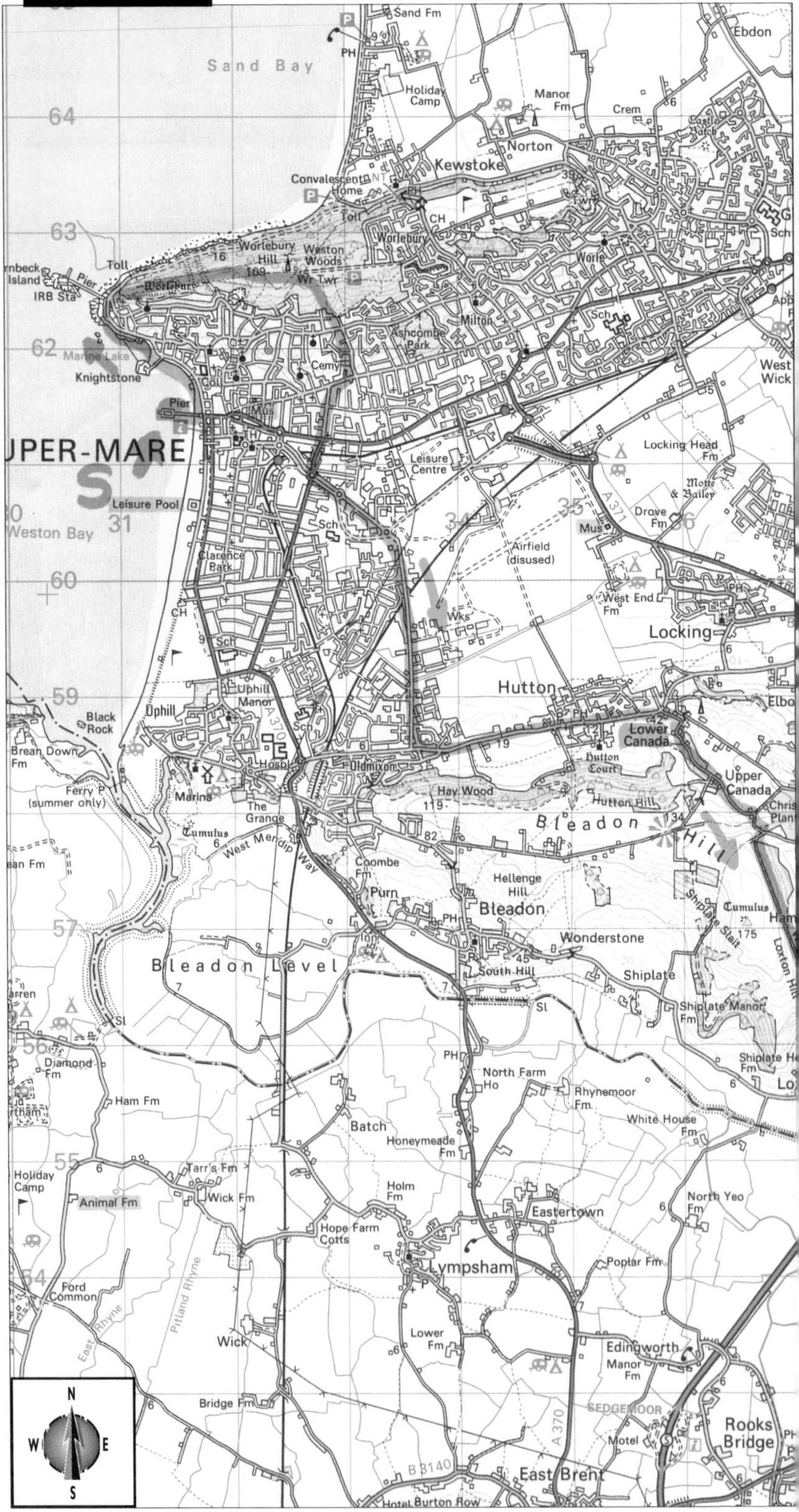

Ebdon

Sand Bay

Holiday Camp

Manor Fm

Crem

Norton

Convalescent Home

Kewstoke

CH

Worlebury

Worlebury Hill 109

Weston Woods

Wr Twr

Worle

nbeck Island

Toll

Worlebury

Toll

Ashcombe Park

Milton

Sch

IRB Sta

Marine Lake

Knightstone

Cemy

West Wick

UPER-MARE

Pier

Locking Head Fm

Leisure Centre

Motte & Bailey

Leisure Pool

Weston Bay

Clarence Park

Sch

Airfield (disused)

Drove Fm

Mus

West End Fm

Locking

CH

Scl

Wks

Uphill Manor

Hutton

Uphill

Sch

Lower Canada

Hutton Court

Upper Canada

Black Rock

Brean Down Fm

Hosp

Oldmixon

Hay Wood

Hutton Hill

Chris Plan

Ferry P (summer only)

Marina

The Grange

Bleadon Hill

Cumulus

West Mendip Way

Coombe

Hellenge Hill

Cumulus 175

an Fm

Purn

Bleadon

Shiplate Slait

Ham

Bleadon Level

Wonderstone

Shiplate

arren

South Hill

Shiplate Manor Fm

Sl

Sl

Shiplate He

Lo

Diamond Fm

PH

North Farm Ho

Rhynemoor Fm

White House Fm

rtham

Ham Fm

Batch

Honeymeade Fm

Holiday Camp

Tarr's Fm

Animal Fm

Wick Fm

Holm Fm

Eastertown

North Yeo Fm

Ford Common

Hope Farm Cotts

Lympsham

Poplar Fm

Wick

Lower Fm

Edingworth

Manor Fm

Bridge Fm

SEDGEMOOR

Rooks Bridge

Motel

B B140

East Brent

Hotel Burton Row

MAP 2

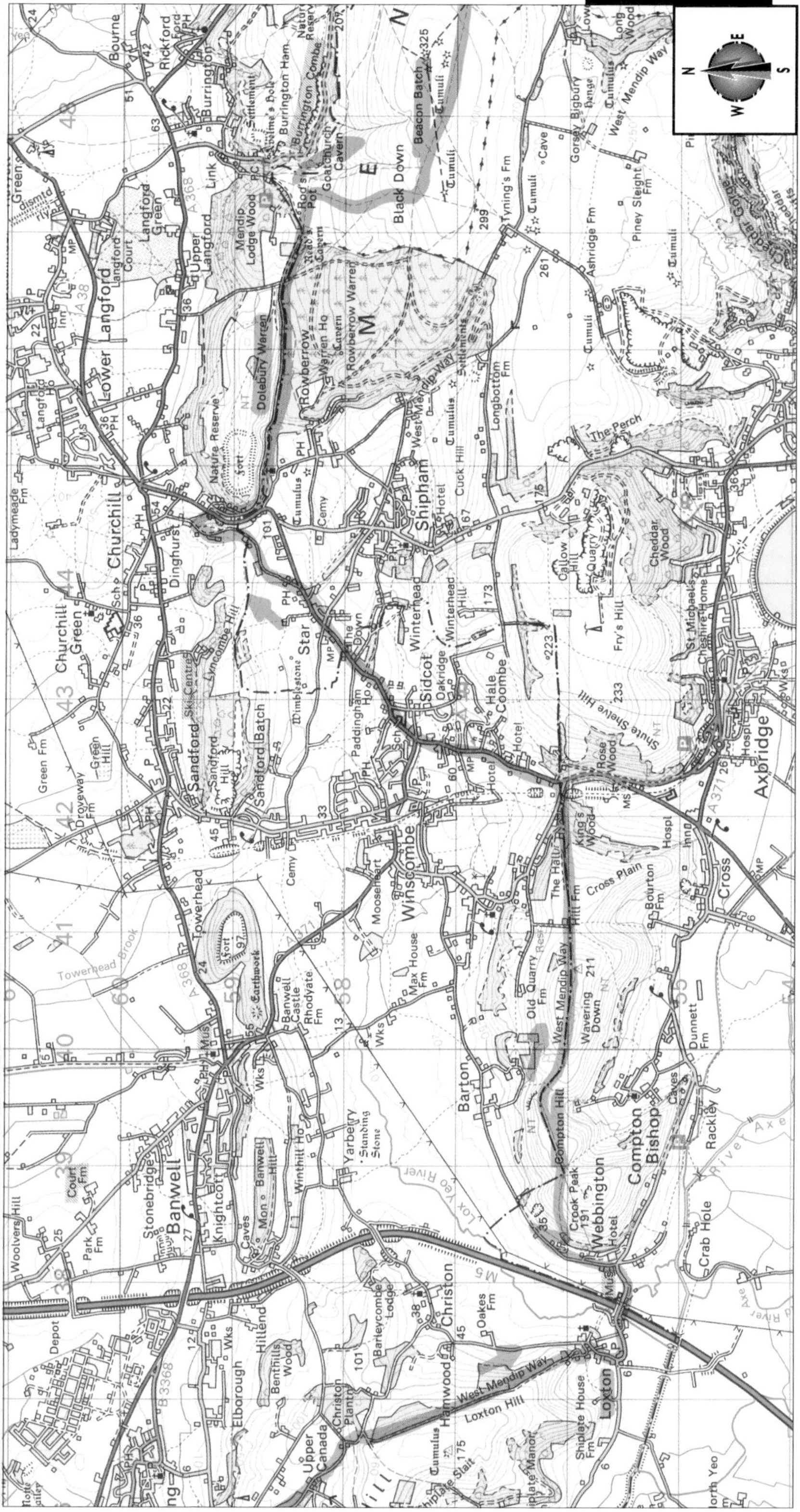
Burrington Combe
Beacon Batch
Black Down
Goatchurch Cavern
Rod's Pot
Burrington
Rickford
Bourne
Upper Langford
Langford Green
Langford Court
Mendip Lodge Wood
Link
Lower Langford
Dolebury Warren
Rowberrow Warren
Rowberrow
West Mendip Way
Tyning's Fm
Ashridge Fm
Piney Sleight Fm
Gorsey Bigbury
Longbottom Fm
Churchill
Churchill Green
Ladymeade Fm
Dinghurst
Nature Reserve
Shipham
Cuck Hill
Winterhead
Winterhead Hill
Sidcot
Oakridge
Star
The Down
Lyncombe Hill
Ski Centre
Sandford
Sandford Hill
Sandford Batch
Wimblestone
Hale Coombe
Callow Hill
Cheddar Wood
Fry's Hill
The Perch
Shute Shelve Hill
Rose Wood
St Michael's Cheshire Home
Axbridge
Cross
King's Wood
Cross Plain
Bourton Fm
Dunnett Fm
Green Fm
Green Hill
Droveway Fm
Towerhead
Towerhead Brook
Winscombe
Mooseheart
Max House Fm
Paddingham Ho
Old Quarry Fm
Hill Fm
The Hall
Wavering Down
Compton Hill
Compton Bishop
Rackley
River Axe
Crab Hole
Crook Peak
Webbington
Barton
Banwell Castle
Rhodyate Fm
Banwell
Banwell Hill
Knightcott
Stonebridge
Court Fm
Woolvers Hill
Park Fm
Winthill Ho
Yarberry
Standing Stone
Lox Yeo River
M5
Christon
Oakes Fm
Barleycombe Lodge
Hillend
Elborough
Benthills Wood
Hamwood
Loxton Hill
Loxton
Shiplate House Fm
Christon Plantn
Upper Canada
Shiplate Manor
Depot
B 3368
A 368
A 38
A 371
North Yeo

MAP I

DAY I Maps I – 4

WESTON TO WELLS
29 miles (47 km) (14 miles (23 km) off-road)
Summits: Worlebury Hill – 109m; Wavering
Down – 211m; Beacon Batch – 325m.

It's barely a few turns of the cranks before you get stuck straight into the first bit of off-road on this 250 mile (402km), channel-to-channel ride: the cobbled climb up Worlebury Hill. Then it's a short, sharp drop into town - beware of the extra weight, things go ballistic extra quick - then suddenly the Mendip Hills loom ahead and there lies the most testing terrain of the trip. High point is Beacon Batch but before that there's a carry - the only one on the Way - onto Combe Hill and some sensational descents and single-track to enjoy.

LOCATION | ROUTE DIRECTIONS

WESTON-S-MARE
From the Grand Pier (GR317614) take Royal Parade road (N) 1m (1.6km) to T-junction then turn L(NE) on Kewstoke Road 0.1m (160m) to fork R(E) up bridleway track into wood for continuous climb 1m (1.6km) to water tower. Fork R(SE) 0.5m (805m) down track then tarmac to crossroads with Manor Road on town edge then go SO(S) 0.3m (483m) to T-junction. Turn R(WSW) on Milton Road 0.15m (241m) to T-junction, turn L(S) on Ashcombe Road, keeping SO(S) to join the A3033 Drove Road, and go 0.5m (805m) to roundabout. Fork L(SE) on Winterstoke Road 1.8m (2.9km), keeping SO(SE) at roundabouts, then turn L(W) off roundabout onto Broadway 1.5m (2.4km), through Hutton up to Lower Canada T-junction.

LOWER CANADA
Turn R(ESE) 1m (1.6km) to go through first T-junction and past Upper Canada to next T-junction then turn R(S then swing SE) 0.1m (160m) up to T-junction and turn R(WSW) for final 110yds (100m) climb to waymarker on T-junction. Turn L(S) down 20yds (18m) through gate then 1.4m (2.25km) down, keeping L on edge of Loxton, to county classified road T-junction. Turn R(S) 0.25m (402m) to T-junction, turn L(S then E), over M5, 0.5m

MAP 2

(805m) then turn L(N) at next T-junction for 0.5m (805m), past "The Paddock" to T-junction with bridleway. Turn R(S then NE) on singletrack behind 'The Paddock', 0.6m (966m) for push/carry up onto Compton Hill.

COMPTON HILL
Keep L(ENE) alongside boundary, 2.2m (3.54km), past Wavering Down trig, Hill Farm and through woods to T-junction then turn R(ESE) 110yds (100m) to the A38 T-junction and turn L(N) 2m (3.22km) to bridleway track just past PH. Fork L(NE) 0.5m (805m) to T-junction then keep R(NE) (manic dogs about!) 0.25m (402m) to take singletrack bridleway off R(SSE) 200yds (183m) down to the A38. Take care, it's a busy road!

DOLEBURY WARREN
Go SO then turn R(SSW) 2.2m (3.54km), up county classified road then through gate(E) onto bridleway track (mud!), through woods to waymarker at bridleway crossroads on open moor. Turn R(S) 0.6m (966m) up to bridleway crossroads then turn L(ESE then E) on track (this doesn't follow map-marked bridleway) 0.8m (1.29km) to Beacon Batch trig.

OFF-ROAD CODE
● **Enjoy the countryside and respect its life and work**

● **Guard against all risk of fire**

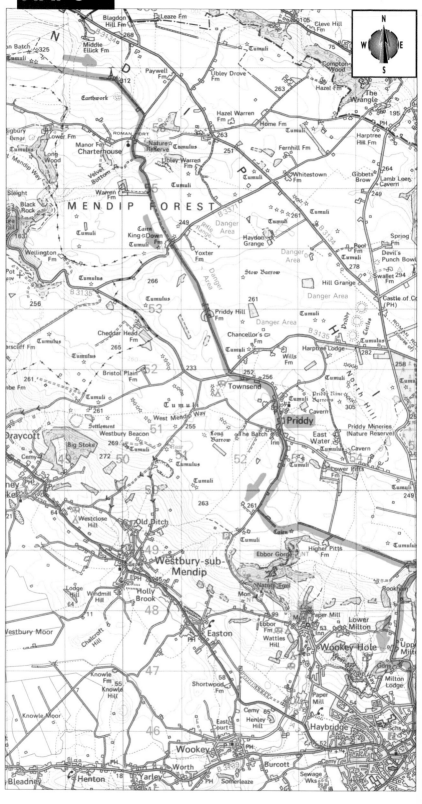

MAP 3

MAP 4

N W E S

Pitcot
Stratton on the Fosse
Moons Hill
Dunford
Holcombe
Hyatt's Hill
Fry's Cave
Stoke St Michael
Waterlip
Dean
Lane Fm
MP
218
Nettlebridge
Wks
Harridge Wood
Stoke Bottom
Batch
Midway
St Michael
Three Ashes
Long Cross
252
Temple House Fm
242
Newman Street
Chelynch
Doulting
211
222
Benter
West Fm
Neighbourne
208
206
Blakes Fm
Lodge Fm
Beacon Fm
Hurlingpot
Ingsdons Hill
Charlton
Oakhill
Ashwick
Badger's Cross
Cemy
Simbriss Fm
Highcroft Fm
248
Beacon Hill
ROMAN ROAD
FOSSE WAY
MENDIP DISTRICT
Bodden
SHEPTON MALLET
ROMAN ROAD
197
Viaduct
Gurney Slade
195
Little London
239
MP
271
A37
Millbrook
Downside
Windsor Hill
Hosl
Cemy
Tumuli
West Shepton
149
Binegar
234
B 3135
243
PH
297
Roemead Fm
CH
296
Warren Fm
Ham Hill
Bowlish
Darshill
Ham Fms
Viaduct
MP
Turner's Court Fm
Tumulus
Ulsasbury or Castle
292
251
Thrupemarsh Fm
dismtdrlly
Burnt House
192
Thrupe
Woods
45
Whitnell Fm
Whitnell Ho
ROMAN ROAD
255
48
49
250
Crapnell Fm
Croscombe
Inn
146
Stump Cross
Whitnell Corner
241
Tumuli
Tumulus
224
Slab House Inn (PH)
Washingpool
Pitts Fm
44
Haydon
226
Wells Hill Bottom Fm
Hill Grove
262
206
372
B 3139
East Horrington
Chilcote Manor
Dinder Wood
Dinder
54
Church Hill
136
dismantled railway
Dungeon
135
Warminster
Tumuli
253
Resr
Hospl
Lyatt
Sharcombe Park
59
Priddy Road Fm
Pen Hill
305
Long Barrow
Prior's Hill
187
Walcombe
Berryl
Knapp Hill
Resr
78
King's Castle
37
Dulcote
Dulcote Hill
A371
Wellesley Fm
31
Twinhills Wood
Hill House Fm
Benge
Tumuli
263
282
Upper Milton
Walcombe
Milton Lodge
Stoberry Park
WELLS
The Park
Schs
Wood
Park
Hill House Fm
249
Tumulus
Cole
Schs
Keward
River
Woodford

BEACON BATCH Keep SO(ESE) 3m (4.83km) on singletrack at first, past mast, then unclassified road down to T-junction, turn R(SSW) then keep SO(S then SSE) over crossroads to staggered crossroads with the B3135. Keep SO(ESE) 2.6m (4.18km), past Priddy, then fork R(S) past PH 0.8m (1.29km) to take bridleway track off L(SE then E) 2m (3.22km) to county classified road. Turn R(S) 2m (3.22km) down (Fast bends, take care!) to crossroads on the A39 on edge of Wells. Turn R to go into town centre for R & R or keep SO(SSE) to continue. **(Suggested overnight stop)**

DAY 2 Maps 4 – 7

WELLS TO WEST LAVINGTON (OR THEREABOUTS)
39 miles (63 km) (19 miles (31 km) off-road)
Summits: Beacon Hill – 288m;
Westbury Hill – 230m; Stoke Hill – 222m.

OK so it's a lot of miles but most of it's on good roads where the distance just disappears beneath those humming tyres. Wells is a beautiful mediaeval city with one of the finest cathedrals in Europe. Go visit the chantry house if you want to see a symphony in stone. Longleat slots in some sensuous single-track and then you're up onto Salisbury Plain for a complete scene change. Pale trails, white chalk tracks and a sunset to ride into if you're lucky.

WELLS After 0.1m (160m) you have to turn L(ENE) (no entry ahead) 0.2m (322m) to T-junction then turn R(S) into Miller Gardens 100yds (91m) then go SO(S) down steps to the B3139 to turn R(SW) 0.1m (160m) to the A371 (keep SO to visit Wells Cathedral). Turn L(SSE) (extremely busy road with heavy lorries!) 0.6m (966m) to track T-junction then fork L(ENE) 0.75m (1.21km), past golf course, to gate. Go through gate then zigzag L/R up to a field then go SO(ESE) 0.8m (1.29km) to gate on unclassified road. Keep SO(E) 0.1m (160m) to go through gate on R into field and swing L(E) 0.5m (805m) across field, through gate then swing R(ESE), to county classified road. Turn L(ENE) 1.6m (2.57km), keep L at next T-junction, up to T-junction below Maesbury Castle.

MAESBURY CASTLE

Turn R(SE) 3.6m (5.79km), keep SO at all crossroads, to T-junction/staggered crossroads where you keep SO(ENE) 3.7m (5.95km) where road swings right down into Rock House hamlet to T-junction on L bend. Turn R(SW) 1.6m (2.57km) (sharp L bend soon!) past Bulls Green and SO(ESE) at T-junction to crossroads. Go SO(ESE) (busy access road to quarry) 0.25m (402m) to T-junction then keep R(SSE) 0.25m (402m) past staggered crossroads in Nunney (castle up L turn, PH over on R) to T-junction.

OFF-ROAD CODE
● **Fasten all gates**
● **Keep dogs under control**

MAP 5

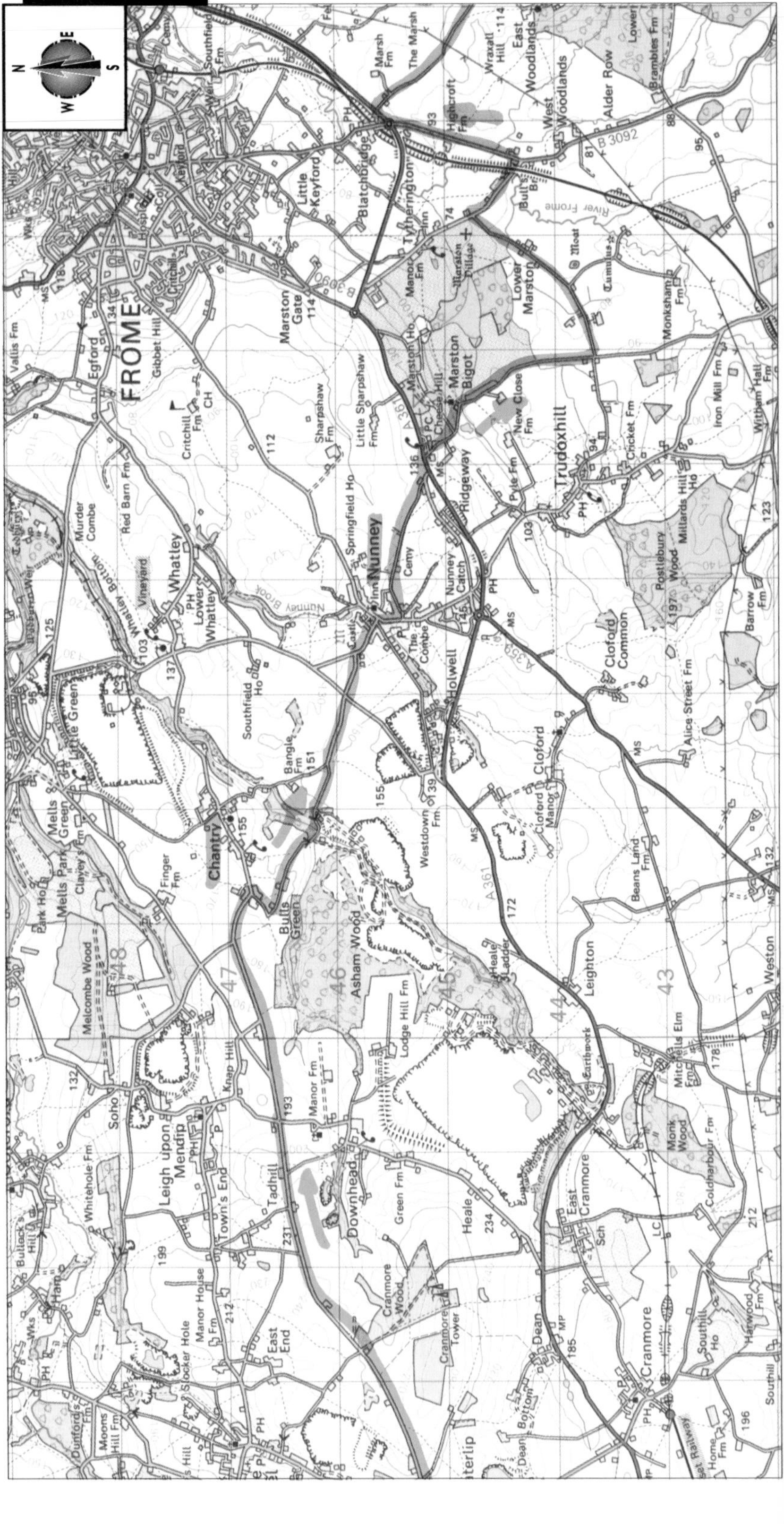

N E S W

FROME

Southfield Fm
Marsh Fm
The Marsh
Wraxall Hill
East Woodlands
West Woodlands
Alder Row
Brambles Wood
Lower

Keyford
Little Keyford
Blatchbridge
Marston Gate
Tytherington
Marston Mead
Marston Bigot
Lower Marston
River Frome
Elliot
Monksham
Iron Mill Fm
Witham Hall
Fm

Vallis Fm
Egford
CH
Gibbet Hill

Critchill Fm CH

Sharpshaw Fm
Little Sharpshaw
Cheese Hill
New Close Fm
Trudoxhill
Cricket Fm

Murder Combe
Red Barn Fm
Whatley
Vineyard
PH
Lower Whatley
Springfield Ho
Nunney
Cemy
Nunney Catch
Ridgeway
Pyle Fm
PH
Postlebury Wood
Barrow Fm

Little Green
Mells Park
Mells
Clavey
Southfield Ho
Castle
The Combe
Holwell
Cloford Common
Alice Street Fm
Clavey

Chantry
Finger Fm
Bangle Fm
Westdown Fm
Cloford
Cloford Manor
Beans Land Fm
Weston

Melcombe Wood
Bull's Green
Asham Wood
Lodge Hill Fm
Heale Ladder
Leighton
Mitchell Elm
Monk Wood

Soho
Knap Hill
Manor Fm
Green Fm
Heale
Earthwork
East Cranmore
Sch
Colcharbour Fm

Leigh upon Mendip
PH
Town's End
Tadhill
Downhead
Heale
Cranmore
Cranmore Tower
Dean
Cranmore
Southill Ho
Southill

Bullock's Hill
Whitehole Fm
Manor House
East End
Cranmore Wood
Dean Bottom
Home Fm
Herwood

Oatford Fm
Moons Hill Fm
PH
WKS
terlip
Rail

MAP 6

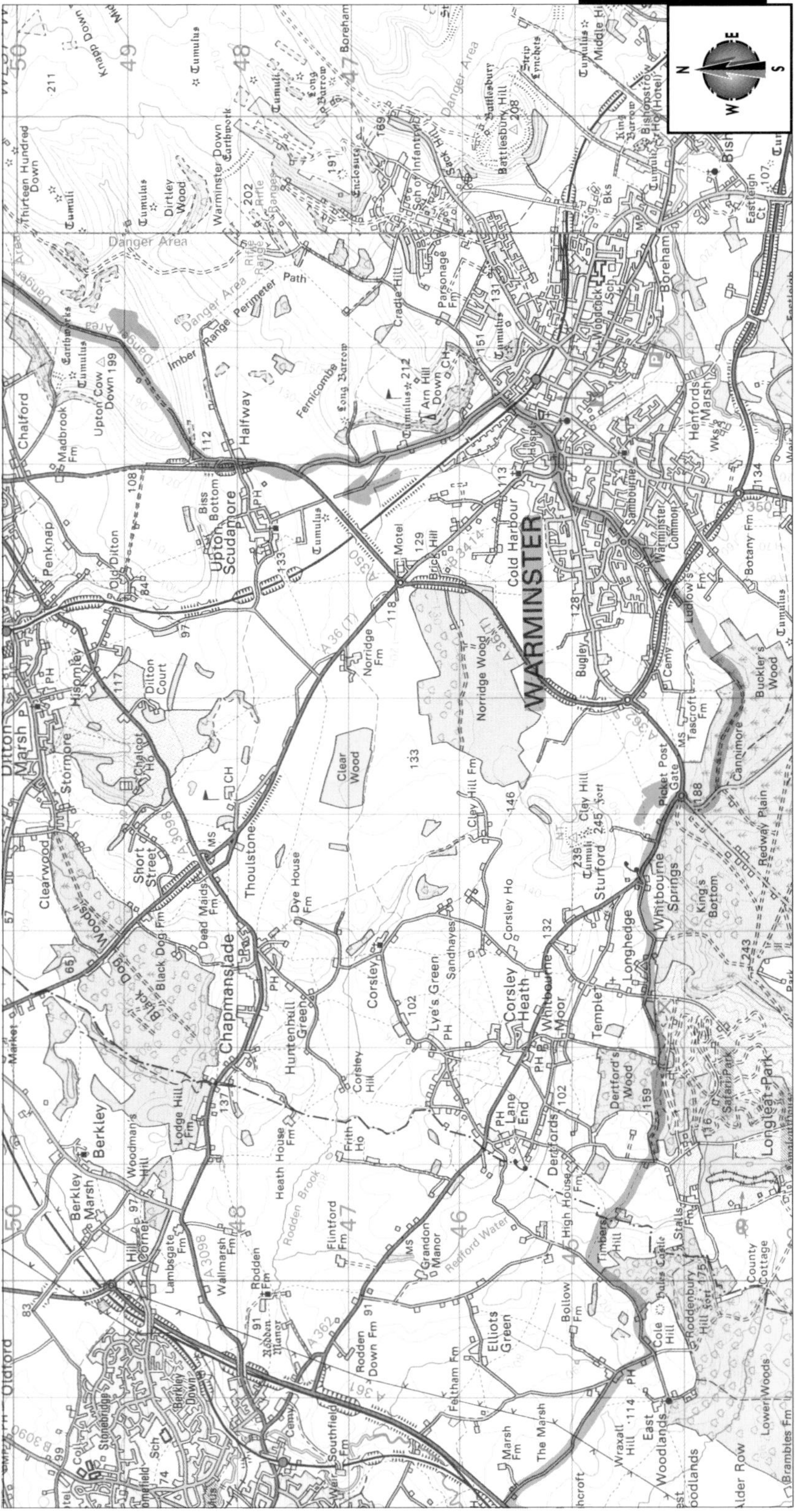

N E S W

Knook Down
211
Thirteen Hundred Down
Tumuli
Dirtley Wood
Warminster Down Earthwork
Danger Area
Chatford
Madbrook Fm
Upton Cow Down 199
Danger Area
Imber Range Perimeter Path
Penknap
Biss Bottom
Upton Scudamore
Old Dilton
Dilton
Dilton Marsh
Hisomley
Stormore
Dilton Court
Chalcot
Short Street
Thoulstone
Clearwood
Dead Maids
Dog Wood
Black Dog Fm
Black Dog Wood
Chapmanslade
Dye House Fm
Huntenhull Green
Corsley
Lye's Green
Market
Berkley
Lodge Hill Fm
Berkley Marsh
Woodman's Hill
Heath House Fm
Frith Ho
Corsley Hill
Hill Corner
Wallmarsh
Lambgate Fm
Rodden
Rodden Brook
Flintford Fm
Grandon Manor
Rodden Down Fm
Hobbs
Oldford
Stonebridge
Berkley Down
Feltham Fm
Elliots Green
Rodden Water
The Marsh
Wraxall Hill 114
Marsh Fm
Bollow
Cole Hill
East Woodlands
Lower Woods
Brambles Fm
Alder Row

Boreham
Battlesbury Hill 208
Strip Lynchets
Middle Hill
Tumulus
King Barrow
Bishopstrow
Eastleigh
Cradle Hill
Parsonage Fm
Long Barrow
Fernicombe
Halfway
Ann Hill
Arn Hill Down
WARMINSTER
Cold Harbour
Motel
Buck Hill
Norridge Fm
Norridge Wood
Warminster Common
Henfords Marsh
Sambourne
Bugley
Clear Wood
Clay Hill Fm
Clay Hill
Cemy
Tascroft Fm
Cannimore
Buckler's Wood
Picket Post Gate
Redway Plain
King's Bottom
Whitbourne Springs
Stourford
Corsley Ho
Whitbourne Moor
Corsley Heath
Sandhayes
Temple
Longhedge
Longleat Park
Lane End
Dertfords
Dertford's Wood
Safari Park
High House Fm
Timber Hill
Hull Castle
Roddenbury Hill 175
County Cottage

NUNNEY Turn R(SSW) 0.1m (160m), then turn L(E) at T-junction 1m (1.6km), keeping L at next T-junction, to staggered crossroads on the A361 where you turn L then turn R(SSE) on lane for 1.25m (2.01km) to staggered crossroads. Turn L(E) 1.1m (1.77km) to T-junction, then turn R(SE) 0.8m (1.29km), under railway, to T-junction for another turn L(NNE) 0.75m (1.21km) up to roundabout on the A361 Frome by-pass (busy road!). Take 3rd exit, A361 (NE), for just 200yds (183m) to T-junction where you turn R(SE) back onto a small lane 1.25m (2.01km) to crossroads there turn L 0.75m (1.21km) to gated track across field at Timbers Hill.

TIMBERS HILL Turn R(ESE) (it's a public footpath so please walk to stream) 0.6m (966m), down to cross stream where bridleway starts, to T-junction with county classified road. Turn R(S) 100yds (91m) to T-junction and turn L(E) onto bridleway track 1m (1.6km), SO(E) at gated T-junction, to join county classified road at crossroads. Keep SO(E) 0.75m (1.21km) to the A362 then turn R(ESE) (busy road with bends so take care when leaving the lane!) 0.5m (805m) to Picket Post Gate. Turn R(SW) to enter Longleat estate for 0.1m (160m) before turn L(SE) 0.15m (241m) down to take concrete then bridleway track off L(E) 1.8m (2.9km), under Warminster by-pass then keep SO at junctions, to county classified road T-junction on the edge of town.

OFF-ROAD CODE
- **Keep to Public Rights of Way across farmland**
- **Use gates and stiles to cross boundaries**

MAP 6

WARMINSTER   Turn L(NW) to roundabout (shops/fish and chips here) then take last exit, to turn R(NE), 0.4m (644m) to T-junction with the former A362 then turn R(E) towards town centre 0.2m (322m) to the B3414. Turn R(E) 0.2m (322m) to town centre T-junction and turn L(NNE) for Westbury 0.5m (805m) to T-junction. Turn L(NW) 1.25m (2.01km) to fork R(N) onto gated 'old road' 0.6m (966m), SO(N) crossroads, to T-junction then fork R(NE) on bridleway, tarmac at first, 2.4m (3.86km) to join county classified road. Go SO(ENE) 0.5m (805m), joining RUPP past car park for White Horse and Bratton Camp, to T-junction. (For Birchanger Farm B&B turn left to B3098 then left again for 1m (1.6 km) to farm.)

OFF-ROAD CODE
- **Leave livestock, crops and machinery alone**
- **Take your litter home**

MAP 7

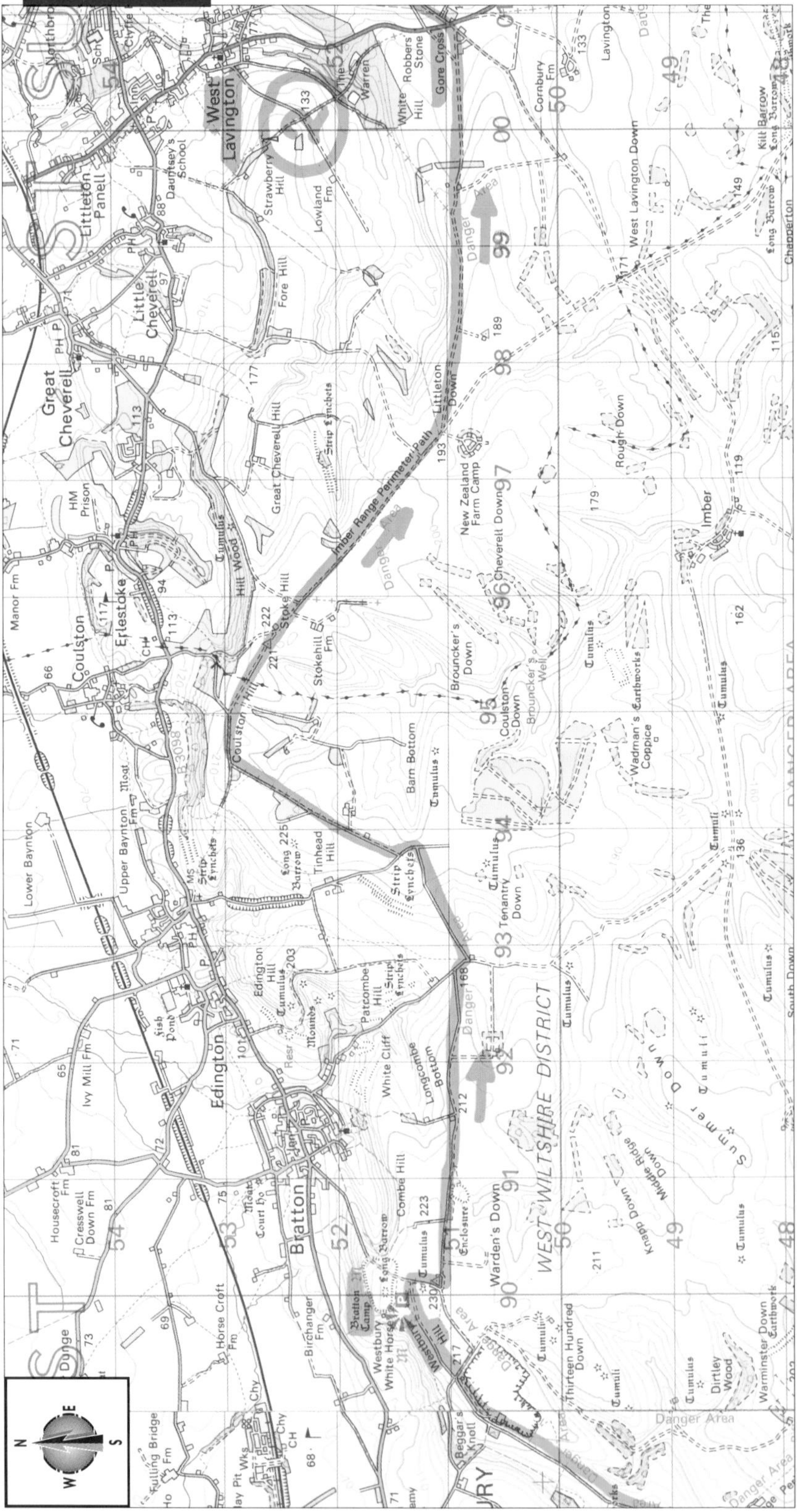

West Lavington
Gore Cross
White Robbers'
Hill Stone
Warren
Cornbury Fm
Lavington
Kill Barrow Long Barrow
Long Barrow
Chapperton
Littleton Panell
Strawberry Hill
Lowland Hill
Fore Hill
Danger
West Lavington Down
Great Cheverell
Daunsey's School
Little Cheverell
New Zealand Farm Camp
Littleton Down
Rough Down
Imber
HM Prison
Great Cheverell Hill
Strip Lynchets
Imber Range Perimeter Path
Cheverell Down
Manor Fm
Hill Wood
Stoke Hill
Stokehill Fm
Brouncker's Down
Wadman's Earthworks Coppice
Erlestoke
Coulston
Barn Bottom
Tumulus
Coulston Down
Brouncker's Well
Lower Baynton
Upper Baynton Fm
Moat
Tinhead Hill
Strip Lynchets
Tenantry Down
Tumulus
Tumuli
DANGER AREA
Coulston
Strip Lynchets
Barrow
Slab Pond
Edington Hill
Patcombe Hill
Mounds
Longcombe Bottom
Danger
Summer Down
WEST WILTSHIRE DISTRICT
Tumuli
Housecroft Fm
Creswell Down Fm
Ivy Mill Fm
White Cliff
Warden's Down
Middle Ridge Down
Kings Down
Tumuli
Dunge
Horse Croft
Horse Croft Fm
Edington
Bratton
Combe Hill
Long Barrow
Enclosure
Tumulus
Thirteen Hundred Down
Dirtley Wood
Warminster Down Earthwork
Birchanger Fm
Bratton Camp
Westbury White Horse
Westbury Hill
Beggar's Knoll
Danger Area
Kallington Bridge
Clay Pit Wks
Chy
CH
Danger Area

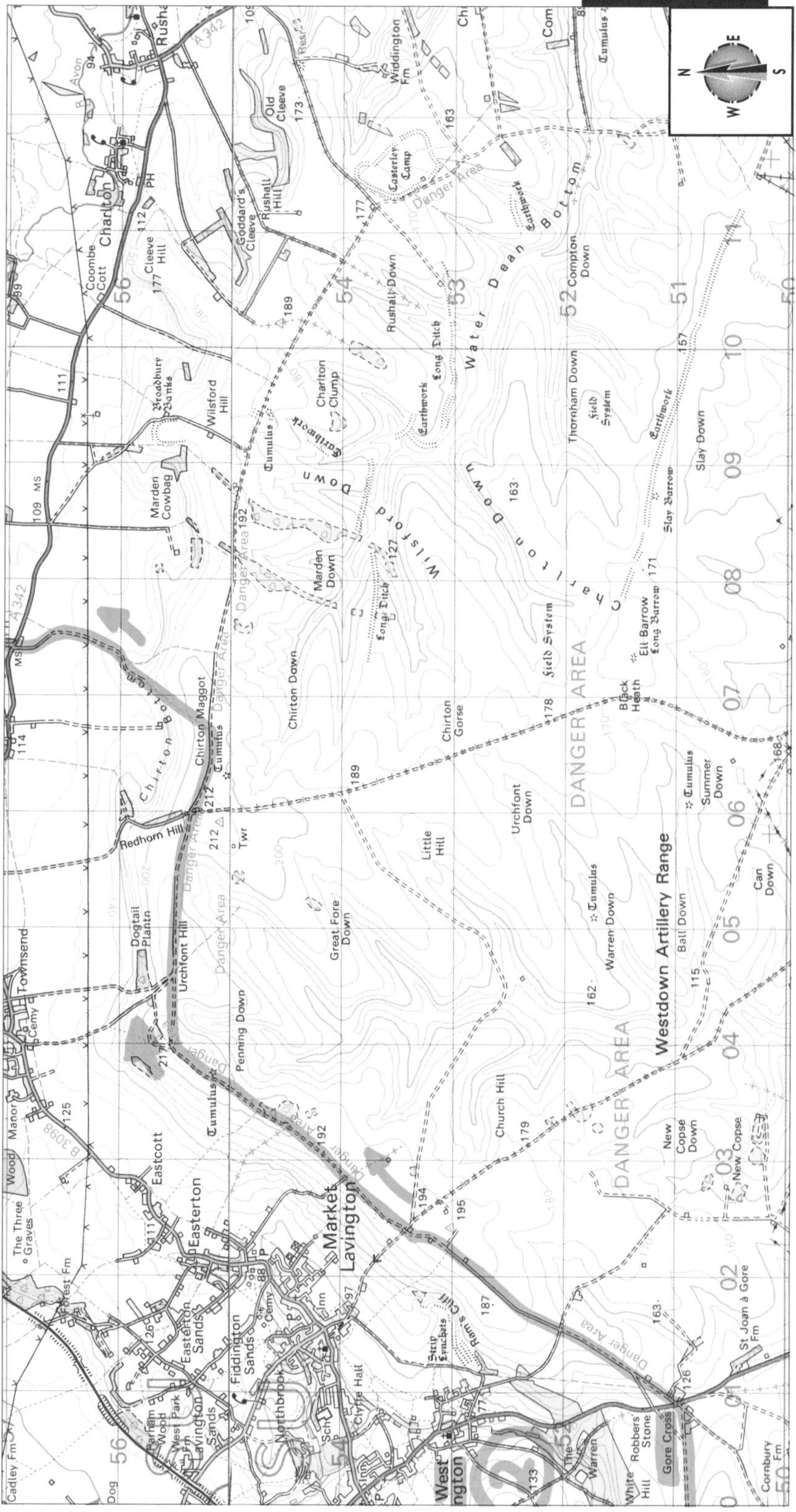

MAP 8

N
W E
S

Rushall

Charlton
Coombe
Cott
Cleeve Hill
Goddard's Cleeve
Old Cleeve

Broadbury Banks
Wilsford Hill

Marden Cowbag

Chirton Bottom

Easterton Camp

Danger Area

Rushall Hill

Charlton Clump
Earthwork

Water Dean Bottom

Thornham Down
Field System

Compton Down

Slay Down
Earthwork

Wilsford Down

Tumulus
Earthwork

Marden Down

Long Ditch

Field System

Earthwork
Long Ditch

Eli Barrow
Long Barrow

Slay Barrow

Chirton Down

Chirton Bottom

Chirton Maggot
Tumulus

Redhorn Hill
212 △ 212
Twr

Dogtail Plantn
Urchfont Hill

Townsend

Chirton Gorse

Black Heath

DANGER AREA

Urchfont Down

Little Hill

Great Fore Down

Penning Down

Tumulus

Summer Down

Can Down

Westdown Artillery Range

Tumulus
Warren Down

Ball Down

DANGER AREA

Wood
Manor

The Three Graves

Eastcott

Easterton

Church Hill

New Copse Down

New Copse

West Fm

Market Lavington

Easterton Sands

Fiddington Sands

Northbrook

Clyffe Hall

Strip Lynchets

St Joan à Gore
Fm

Lavington Sands

White Robbers Hill Stone
Gore Cross

Conbury Fm

West ington

The Warren

MAP 7

**BRATTON
CAMP**

Turn R(S) 0.2m (322m) up to White Horse Farm then turn L(E) 1.75m (2.82km) to T-junction. Turn R(SE) 200yds (183m) to T-junction at military check point then turn L(ENE) 0.75m (1.21km). At T-junction turn L(N) 200yds (183m) and fork R(NNE) 1m (1.6km) to another T-junction where you turn R(E) 2.4m (3.86km) to crossroads near New Zealand Farm Camp and fork L(E) 2.4m (3.86km) to the A360 at Gore Cross. **(Suggested overnight stop)**

OFF-ROAD CODE

● **Do not contaminate water**

● **Protect wild flora and fauna**

DAY 3 Maps 8 – 11

WEST LAVINGTON TO COLLINGBOURNE KINGSTON

**29 miles (47 km) (21 miles (34 km) off-road)
Summits: Redhorn Hill – 212m; Golden Ball
Hill – 268m; Fyfield Down – 233m.**

If the weather's fine today's a peach. Brilliant off-roading with a
scenic saunter on the far side of Pewsey Vale and pedestrian-free,
fast-track downhills to gratify your gravity suck. The climb up
Fyfield's a calf-searing experience but then the roller-coaster run
to Collingbourne topped off by a stop at the Old School House
pasta palace will end a day to remember. Mind you the mud plug
below Aughton has claimed one or two Range Rovers before now!

GORE CROSS Go SO(NNE) onto county classified road 2m
(3.22km) to crossroads with tracks. Keep
SO(NNE) on RUPP track 1.75m (2.82km) then
swing R(E) 1.75m (2.82km), keeping SO(ESE) at
building, to turn L(N) on bridleway track 1.5m
(2.4km), keeping L(NW) at fork down in valley, to
crossroads with the A342. Go SO(N) 3m
(4.83km), to All Cannings where there's a PH and
shop.

OFF-ROAD CODE
- Take special care on country
  roads
- Make no unnecessary noise

MAP 9

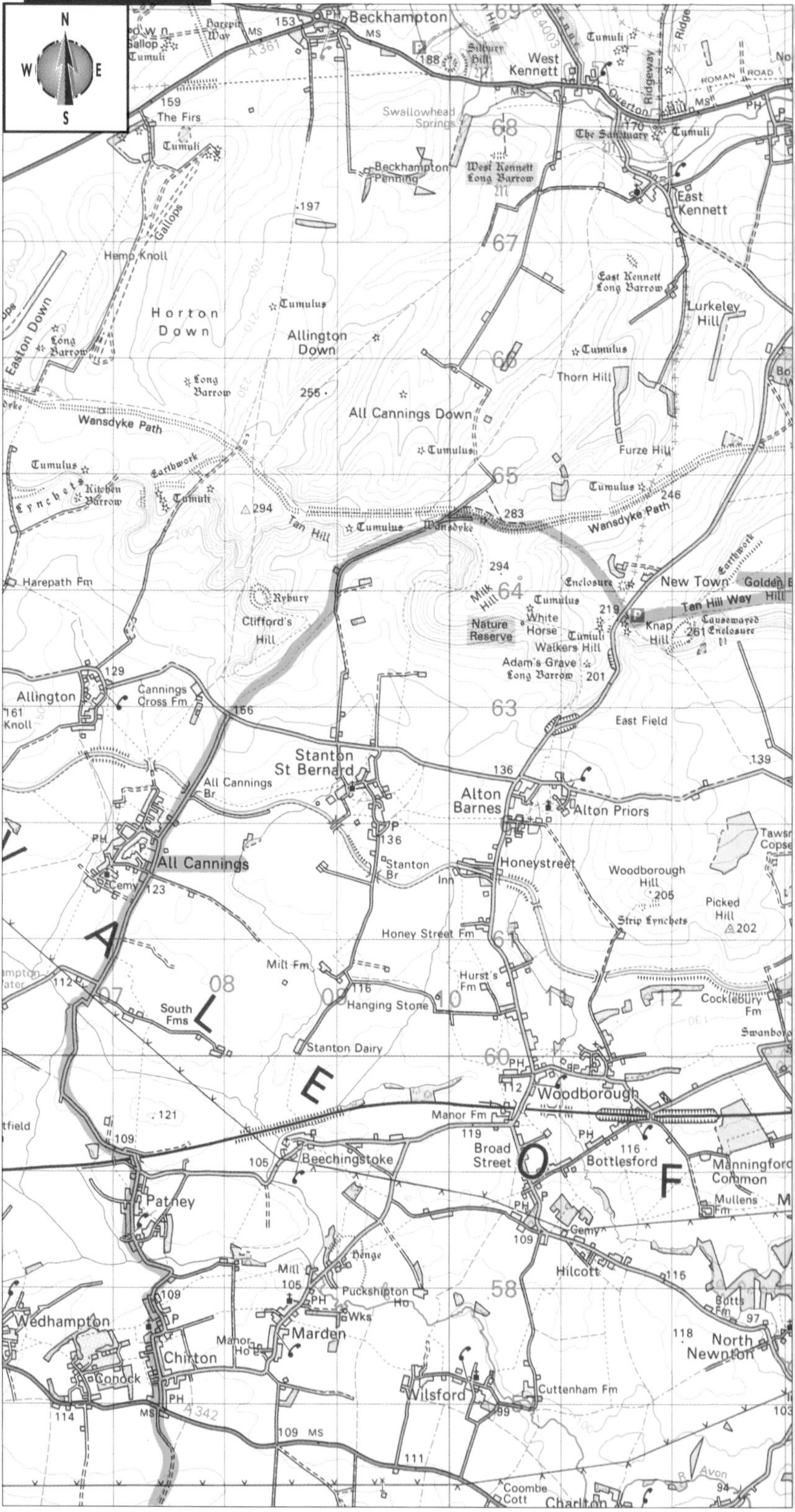

N
W E
S

Down n
Gallop
Tumuli
Harepin
Way

153

MS

Beckhampton

Silbury
Hill

West
Kennett

188
P

A 361

A 4361

A 4

ROMAN
ROAD

No

Overton Ridgeway

NT

159
The Firs

Tumuli

68

Swallowhead
Springs

MS

The Sanctuary

Tumuli

PH

Beckhampton
Penning

West Kennett
Long Barrow

211

East
Kennett

197

67

East Kennett
Long Barrow

Lurkeley
Hill

246

Hemp Knoll

Tumulus

Easton Down

Horton
Down

Long
Barrow

Allington
Down

66

Thorn Hill

Tumulus

Bo

Dyke

Long
Barrow

255

All Cannings Down

Furze Hill

Wansdyke Path

Tumulus

65

Tumulus

Wansdyke Path

Tumulus
Lynchets
Kitchen
Barrow

Earthwork

Tumuli

△ 294

Tan Hill

Tumulus
Wansdyke

283

Enclosure

Earthwork

New Town

Golden B
Hill

Harepath Fm

Rybury

294

Milk
Hill

64

White
Horse

Tumulus

219

Knap
Hill

Tan Hill Way

Causewayed
261 Enclosure

Clifford's
Hill

Nature
Reserve

Tumuli
Walkers Hill

Adam's Grave
Long Barrow

201

129

Cannings
Cross Fm

156

63

East Field

.139

161
Knoll

Allington

**Stanton
St Bernard**

136

Tawsi
Copse

All Cannings
Br

**Alton
Barnes**

Alton Priors

PH

P

Stanton
Br

136

Honeystreet

Woodborough
Hill
.205

Picked
Hill
△202

All Cannings

Cemy

23

Inn

Strip Lynchets

112

07

08

Mill Fm

00

116

Honey Street Fm

61

Hurst's

10

11

Cocklebury
Fm

12

South
Fms

Hanging Stone

Stanton Dairy

L E

60

PH

Swanbo

112

Woodborough

121

Manor Fm

hampton
ater

109

105

Beechingstoke

119

Broad
Street

PH

O F

116

Bottlesford

116

Manningfor
Common

Mullens

M

Patney

109

Cemy

Hilcott

115

Mill

105

Drange

PH

58

Butts
Fm

97

109

Wedhampton

PH

Puckshipton
Ho

Wks

118

North
Newnton

Manor

Marden

103

Chirton

Conock

PH

114

MS

A 342

109

MS

Wilsford

Cuttenham Fm

99

111

94

R Avon

Coombe
Cott

Charlton

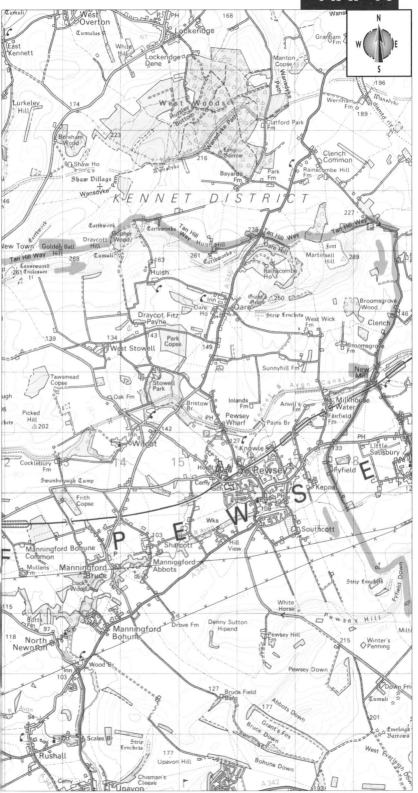

MAP 10

ALL CANNINGS SO(NNE) 1.5m (2.4km) to bridleway/county classified road crossroads. Keep SO(NE) through gate onto RUPP singletrack 1m (1.6km) to T-junction then swing L(N) on track 1m (1.6km), climbing all the way and keeping R at forks to a field. Turn L(ESE), parallel with Wansdyke on your L(N), 0.2m (322m) then dip down L(N) to go through bridleway gate. Then turn R(ESE) 0.75m (1.21km), following field boundary on your R(SW) on track/path that's faint at times through two gates to crossroads with county classified road. Go SO(SE) on RUPP 0.1m (160m) then turn L(E) through gate up singletrack bridleway 0.25m (402m) to gate on Golden Ball Hill.

GOLDEN BALL HILL Go SO(ENE then E) through gate, up onto hilltop where singletrack disappears, 1m (1.6km) roughly following ridge edge, through two gates to waymarker. Fork L(NE) 0.1m (160m) across to gate. Go SO(ENE) through gate 0.6m (966m), on track and SO(E) at crossroads in valley bottom, up to T-junction. Turn R(S then ESE) on obvious, gated bridleway 0.75m (1.21km) to Huish Hill house to turn L(NE then soon after E) on bridleway track 0.6m (966m) to the A345. Go SO(S then soon after E) 0.5m (805m) then turn L(NE) on field edge 0.4m (644m) to zigzag L/R and follow singletrack bridleway on top of embankment 0.1m (160m) to gate. Go SO(E) through gate 50yds (46m) to then swing L(NE) then swing R(E) round copse, across field to go along S side of next copse 0.5m (805m) to county classified road. Turn R(ESE) 1.25m (2.01km) to T-junction then fork R(SSW) 0.75m (1.21km) to T-junction in New Mill. **(for Wet Weather Route avoiding muddy Fyfield route keep SO, see page 57)**

NEW MILL Turn R(SW) 0.8m (1.29km) to staggered crossroads on the B3087 then zigzag R/L to keep SO(SSW) 1m (1.6km), through Fyfield then on bridleway track (mud bath when wet!), over stream then across field keeping boundary on your R(W), to join singletrack bridleway beneath power lines. Keep SO(SSE) 0.5m (805m), passing right by barn and windpump, to pick up bridleway track at foot of ridge. Swing L(ENE) for 0.6m (966m) climb up to field corner then turn R(SW) 0.2m (322m) by fence then hairpin L(NE) through gate and back on far side of fence for 0.1m (160m). Swing R(SSE) 0.4m (644m) to track crossroads, turn L(NNE) (muddy stretch here, if wet) 0.8m (1.29km) to T-junction in valley bottom below Easton Hill.

WET WEATHER ROUTE FROM NEW MILL. Keep SO(SSE) 0.7m (1.13km) to the B3087 crossroads, keep SO(S) 1.6m (2.57km), through Milton Lilbourne to fork L by Priory Cottage and under power lines then track does lazy swing L/R up ridge, to T-junction in valley. Keep SO(SSE) past barn below Easton Hill to continue.

OFF-ROAD CODE
● **Cycle only on permitted Rights of Way**
● **Give way to horse riders and walkers**

MAP 11

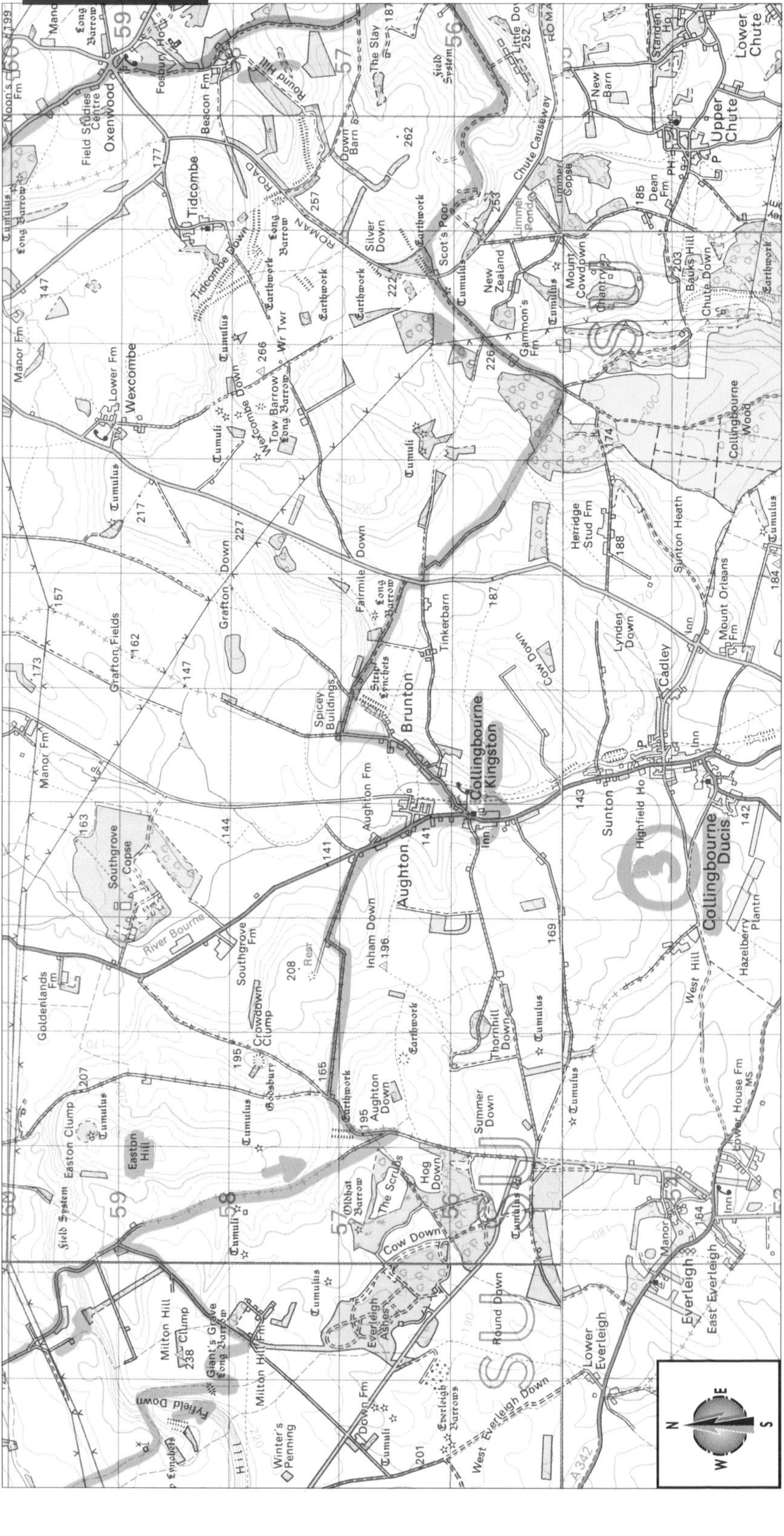

Noon's Fm, Manor, Long Barrow, Field Studies Centre, Oxenwood, Fosbury, Round Hill, The Slay, Field System, ROMAN, Lower Chute, Upper Chute, Starden, New Barn, Chute Causeway, Tidcombe, Beacon Fm, Down Barn, Silver Down, Scot's Poor, Earthwork, New Zealand, Mount Cowdown, Conholt, Dean, Banks Hill, Chute Down, Earthwork, Manor Fm, Lower Fm, Wexcombe, Tidcombe Down, Long Barrow, Wr Twr, Tow Barrow, Long Barrow, Wexcombe Down, Tumuli, Gammon's Fm, Tumulus, Collingbourne Wood, Herridge Stud Fm, Sunton Heath, Grafton Down, Fairmile Down, Long Barrow, Tinkerbarn, Cow Down, Lynden Down, Mount Orleans, Cadley, Grafton Fields, Spicey Buildings, Brunton, Collingbourne Kingston, Sunton, Highfield Ho, Collingbourne Ducis, Hazelberry Plantn, Manor Fm, Southgrove, Southgrove Copse, Aughton Fm, Aughton, Inham Down, Rear, Crowdown Clump, River Bourne, Goldenlands, Easton Clump, Easton Hill, Cobury, Inham Down, Thornhill Down, West Hill, Lower House Fm, Field System, Tumulus, Aughton Down, Summer Down, Oblat Barrow, The Scrubs, Hog Down, Cow Down, East Everleigh, Everleigh, Milton Hill Clump, Giant's Grave, Long Barrow, Milton Hill Fm, Everleigh Wood, Round Down, Lower Everleigh, Fyfield Down, Winter's Penning, Down Fm, Everleigh Barrows, Everleigh Down, West Everleigh Down

Elevation markers: 199, 59, 57, 56, 252, 177, 262, 257, 253, 185, 222, 226, 203, 266, 174, 147, 217, 227, 188, 157, 162, 147, 173, 187, 143, 142, 163, 144, 141, 169, 196, 208, 207, 195, 165, 238, 201, 342

MAP 12

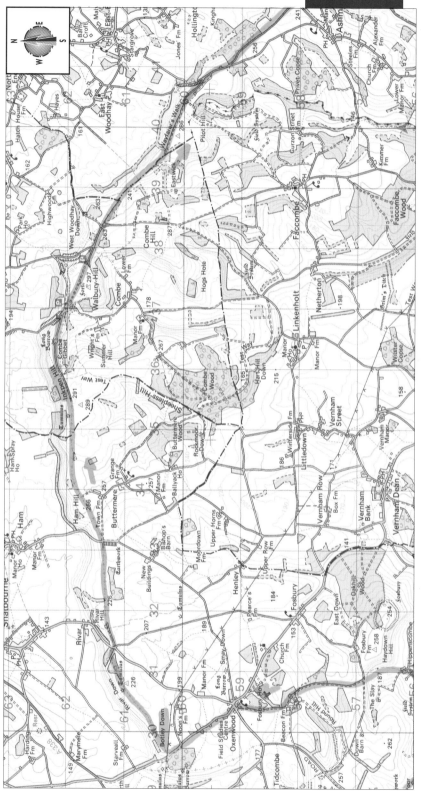

MAP 11

EASTON HILL Turn R(SSE) 1.75m (2.82km), past barn, on bridleway track (can get muddy in valley) finally to climb to T-junction, turn L(N) here 0.5m (805m) down to 'Black Barn' T-junction. Turn R(E) 1.5m (2.4km), turning R(ESE) at T-junction by another barn, to the A338. Turn R(SSE) 0.6m (966m) to T-junction by Collingbourne Kingston church. **(Suggested overnight stop)**

DAY 4 Maps 11 – 14

COLLINGBOURNE TO DEANE (OR THEREABOUTS)
**33 miles (53 km) (25 miles (40 km) off-road)
Summits: Rivar Hill – 226m; Walbury Hill – 297m; Ladle Hill – 234m.**

Today we leave the Plain behind and hook up on an ancient ridge route beginning with Rivar Down. But before that you're treated to a curious fold in the hills called Hippenscombe Bottom where an idle llama or two might be stirred to exchange looks as you speed by. Up on Rivar your hard-won height commands fantastic views culminating with Gibbet Combe. It's here that the Wessex Way joins forces with the Wayfarer's Walk all the way to the foot of Winchester Hill. Watch out for walkers! The Way quits the escarpment with a bevy of downhill blasts before heading into the heart of Hampshire and Deane.

COLLING-BOURNE K. Turn L(NE) 1m (1.6km) to T-junction at Spicey Buildings then turn R(ESE) 1m (1.6km), keeping SO(ESE) at next T-junction, to county classified road. Turn R(S) then almost immediately turn L(E) onto track then almost immediately fork R(SE) on bridleway track with gates 1.5m (2.4km), across valley and straight through woods, to RUPP track crossroads. Turn L(NE) 1m (1.6km) to crossroads with county classified road at Scot's Poor then go SO(E) onto singletrack bridleway hard by L(N) side of cottage 2m (3.22km) along meandering valley bottom to Hippenscombe Farm T-junction.

HIPPENS-COMBE Turn L(NNW) on RUPP 125yds (114m) through farm then fork R(NNE) just in front of barn for

0.5m (805m) climb to crossroads, go SO(NNW) 1m (1.6km) to T-junction at Beacon Farm then turn R(N) on tarmac drive 0.5m (805m) to Oxenwood. Swing L(NW), beside village green, 1m (1.6km) to turn R(ENE) through gate onto bridleway track along the edge of Botley Down 1.4m (2.25km) to county classified road and then zigzag R/L to continue on bridleway track 1.2m (1.93km) to crossroads with county classified road. Go SO(E) then immediately fork L(ENE) back onto bridleway track over Ham Hill and 2m (3.22km) to track T-junction (a muddy spot in the wet) on Inkpen Hill.

INKPEN HILL Swing L(ENE) 0.8m (1.29km), past Gibbet to crossroads with county classified road; (extensive panoramas from here and where the long distance Wayfarer's Walk begins. This walk and the Wessex Way share bridleways, but not footpaths, for much of the time until Hinton Ampner. The distinctive 'WW' waymarker is a useful confirmation that you're on the right track). Continue SO(ESE) on bridleway track 1m (1.6km), joining county classified road on bend, to staggered crossroads. Zigzag L/R, effectively SO(ESE), back onto bridleway track 0.9m (1.45km) to swing L(ESE) 0.9m (1.45km) to join county classified road and there turn R(SSE) 0.4m (644m) to fork L(SE) on bridleway track (muddy stretch when wet). 1m (1.6km) to another staggered crossroads. Here zigzag R/L, effectively SO(ESE) 0.6m (966m) to the A343 junction. Zigzag L/R/L, effectively SO(ESE), to continue on bridleway track 1.5m (2.4km), past Highclere gate-house, to T-junction on descent just beyond the line of trees on Upper Woodcott Down.

MAP 13

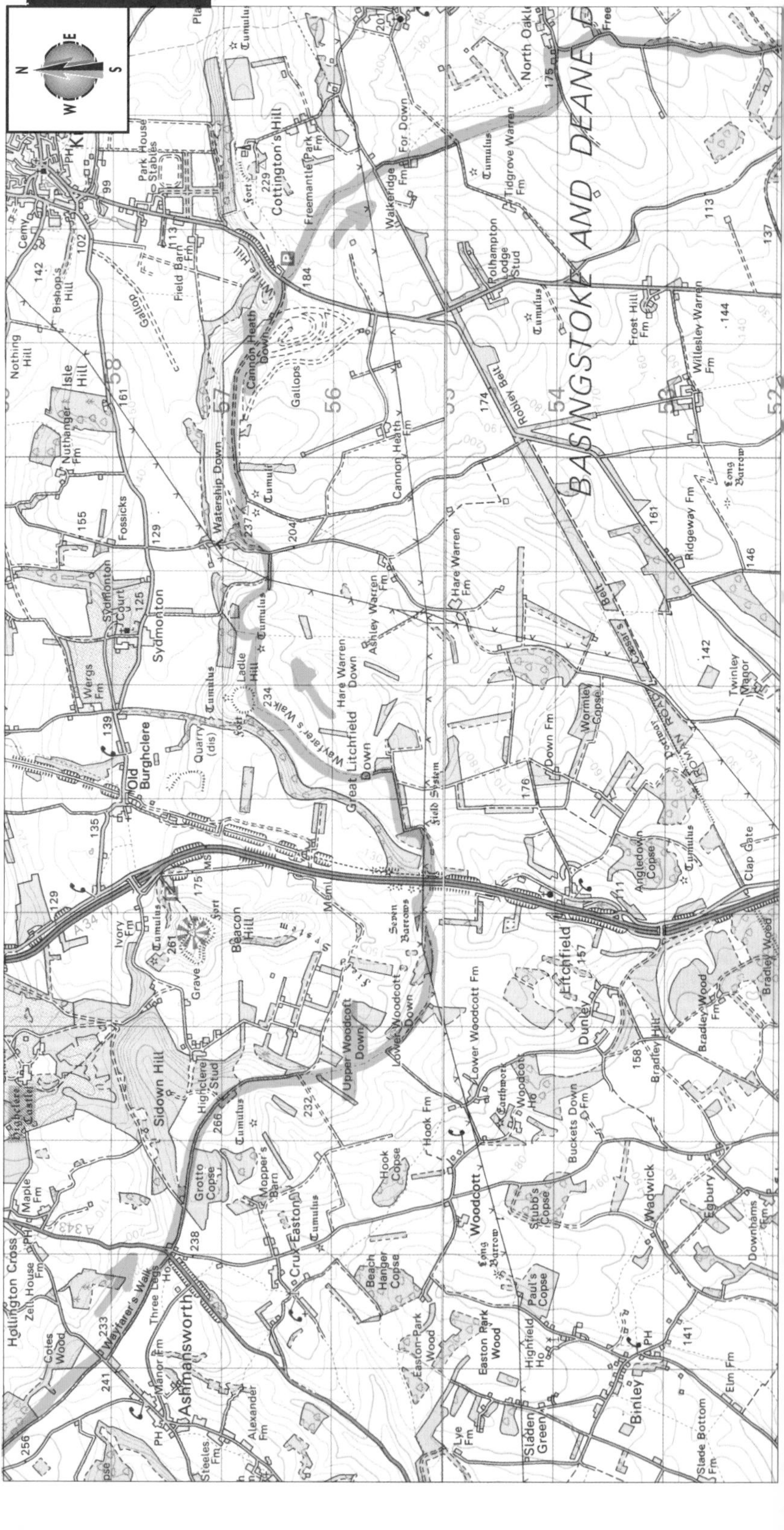

Wayfarer's Walk
Ashmansworth
Hollington Cross
Zell House Fm
Maple Fm
Coles Wood
Manor Fm
Three Legs Ho
Alexander Fm
Steeles Fm
Highclere Castle
Sidown Hill
Highclere Stud
Grotto Copse
Mopper's Barn
Crux Easton
Beacon Hill
Ivory Fm
Grave
Upper Woodcott Down
Lower Woodcott Down
Seven Barrows
Old Burghclere
Quarry (dis)
Wergs Fm
Sydmonton Court
Sydmonton
Fossicks
Nuthanger Fm
Nothing Hill
Isle Hill
Bishop's Hill
Field Barn Fm
Park House Stables
Ladle Hill
Great Litchfield Down
Hare Warren Down
Ashley Warren Fm
Hare Warren Fm
Watership Down
Cannon Heath Down
Gallops
Cannon Heath Fm
White Hill
Cottington's Hill
Freemantle Park Fm
For Down
Walkeridge Fm
Tidgrove Warren Fm
North Oakley
Polhampton Lodge Stud
Robley Belt
Caesar's Belt
BASINGSTOKE AND DEANE
Frost Hill Fm
Willesley Warren Fm
Ridgeway Fm
Twinley Manor
Wormley Copse
Down Fm
Angledown Copse
Clap Gate
Litchfield
Dunley
Bradley Wood
Bradley Wood Fm
Bradley Hill
Lower Woodcott Fm
Woodcott Ho
Buckets Down Fm
Hook Fm
Hook Copse
Woodcott
Stubb's Copse
Wadwick
Egbury
Downhams Fm
Beach Hanger Copse
Easton Park Wood
Paul's Copse
Highfield Ho
Sladen Green
Lye Fm
Binley
Slade Bottom Fm
Elm Fm
Long Barrow
Tumulus
A343
A34

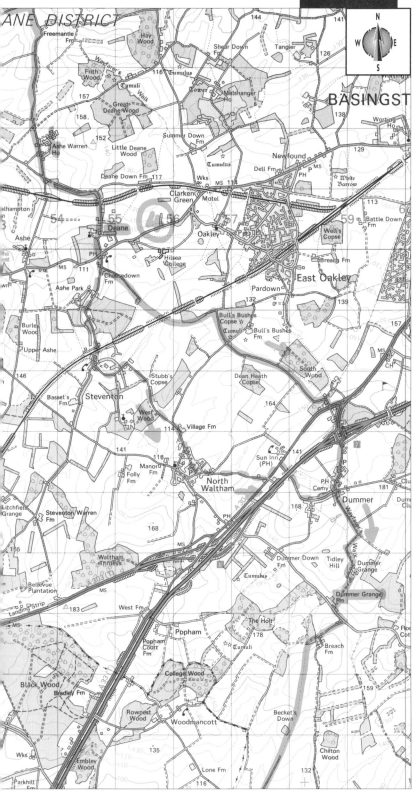

MAP 14

ANE DISTRICT

Freemantle
Fm

Hay
Wood

Shear Down
Fm

Tangier

144

141

126

N
W E
S

Wayfarer's

Frith
Wood

116

Tumulus

Walk

Tumuli

Tower

Matshanger
Ho

120

BASINGST

157

Great
Deane Wood

158.

152

Ashe Warren
Ho

Little Deane
Wood

Summer Down
Fm

Tumulus

Newfound

Dell Fm

PH

MS

138

Worting
Ho

129

White
Barrow

Deane Down Fm 117

Wks

MS 114

Clarken
Green

Motel

54

55

56

57

59

113

Battle Down
Fm

60

lhampton

Ashe

Deane

Oakley

PH

P

Well's
Copse

he
st

MS

111

Cheesedown
Fm

Hilsea
College

Breach Fm

East Oakley

61

wrP

Ashe Park

Pardown

132

139

Burley
Wood

Bull's Bushes
Copse

157

Upper Ashe

Tumuli

Bull's Bushes
Fm

MS

CH

146

Stubb's
Copse

Dean Heath
Copse

South
Wood

Basset's
Fm

Steventon

West
Wood

164

141

114

Village Fm

116

Manor
Fm

Folly
Fm

North
Waltham

Sun Inn
(PH)

141

7

P

Litchfield
Grange

Steventon Warren
Fm

PH

Cemy

181

Dummer

Clu

Dum
Clu

168

PH

168

Wayfarer's

155

Waltham
Trinleys

MS

Dummer Down
Fm

Tidley
Hill

Walk

Dummer
Grange

Bellevue
Plantation

183

West Fm

Tumuli

Dummer Grange
Fm

Landing Strip

MS

The Holt

Flo
Cot

Popham

178

Breach
Fm

Black
Wood

Bradley Fm

Popham
Court
Fm

College Wood

159

Rowpest
Wood

Woodmancott

Becket's
Down

Chilton
Wood

Wks

135

Embley
Wood

Lone Fm

116

132

Parkhill

UPPER WOODCOTT

Fork R(S) (easy to overshoot!) up across field on faint singletrack at first, 1.6m (2.57km) and SO(SE) at gated T-junction then swing R(ESE) on exiting woods for final run to the A34. Go SO(E) (it's a very busy road!) under rail bridge up tarmac singletrack bridleway 0.8m (1.29km), swinging L(N) then turning R(E), to T-junction. Turn L(N) on bridleway track then singletrack 1.5m (2.4km), over Ladle Hill to bridle-gate after L bend. Turn R(E) through gate, swinging R(SE) along field top 0.4m (644m), through gate and then on bridleway track to county classified road. Go SO(NE) 1.8m (2.9km) up bank on singletrack bridleway at first, round the top of Watership Down then down to the B3051 crossroads at Cannon Heath.

CANNON HEATH

Zigzag L/R, effectively SO(SE), over hill 0.8m (1.29km) to staggered crossroads with county classified road then keep SO(SSE) on tarmac bridleway at first 0.5m (805m), past Walkeridge farm, to crossroads. Keep SO(SSE) on singletrack bridleway over pasture 0.6m (966m) to T-junction then turn L(ENE) 0.25m (402m) to T-junction with county classified road in North Oakley. Turn R(S) 1.9m (3.06km), past Ash Warren House, to swing L(ESE) at staggered crossroads 0.6m (966m) then R(SSE) at T-junction and 0.6m (966m) to

crossroads with the B3400 in Deane. **(Suggested overnight stop)**

OFF-ROAD CODE
● **Do not ride in such a manner that you are a danger to others**

DAY 5 Maps 14 – 17

DEANE TO BURITON
34 miles (55 km) (23 miles (38 km) off-road)
Summits: Wether Down – 234m;
Butser Hill – 270m.

Pay attention to the wet weather routes as today is a mud-plugger's delight. After a good dry spell there's surprisingly little gloop but deal out a downpour or two and you're in for some traction-testing mire! If it's summer you'll have learnt a thing or two about stingers, grass-whipping and ruts. New Alresford is a quaint, ancient town with all the modcons for a mid-trip restock. Today has a sting in it's tail - the South Downs. Climbs are calf-searingly steep but then the descents are demonic. Off Winchester Hill we hook up with the South Downs Way. The upside is that it's superbly signed and we're onto more all-weather tracks, the downside is that it can get busy so take other trail users into account when you put the pedal down. From the junction with the county classified road at Fagg's Farm drop left into Buriton - you've got a choice of tarmac or track.

DEANE (For Wet Weather Route to Dummer avoiding mud keep SO, see below)
Go SO(S) 0.1m (160m) then turn L(ESE) onto RUPP track 1.5m (2.4km) (it is usually extremely muddy under the rail bridge) to T-junction with county classified road and there turn R(SSE) 1.7m (2.74km) to the A30 at Oakdown (this is a busy junction so take care as you have to cross to the far side of the eastbound lane to continue). Turn L(ENE) (heading for M3 and Dummer) 150yds (137m) then fork R and then swing R(S) 0.2m (322m) to roundabout to go SO(S) on 2nd exit 0.7m (1.13km), past PO, to staggered crossroads in Dummer.

WET WEATHER ROUTE FROM DEANE TO DUMMER.
Keep SO(S) 1.3m (1.93km) to T-junction in Steventon, to turn L(SE) 1.6m (2.57km), keeping SO(SE) at next T-junction, to T-junction on outskirts of North Waltham. Fork L(SSE) 0.3m (483m) to T-junction then turn

MAP 15

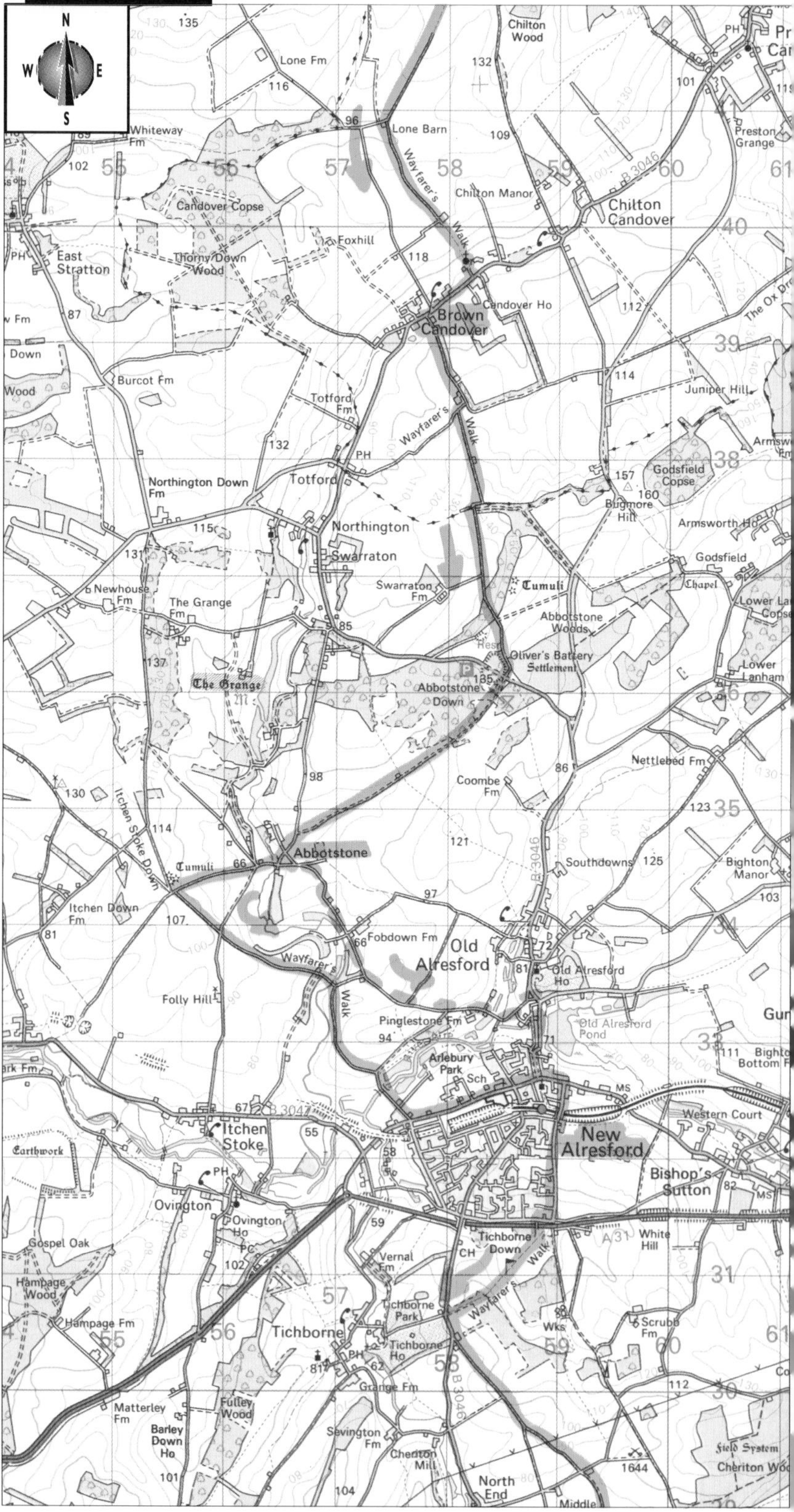

N
W E
S

135
Chilton Wood
PH
Pr
Ca
Lone Fm
132
116
101
119
96
Lone Barn
109
B 3046
Preston
Grange
102
55
55
57
58
59
60
61
Candover Copse
Chilton Manor
Chilton
Candover
40
Foxhill
118
East
Stratton
PH
Thorny Down
Wood
Brown
Candover
Candover Ho
112
The Ox Dr
39
87
Down
114
Juniper Hill
Wood
Burcot Fm
Armsw
Totford
Fm
157
Godsfield
38
160
Copse
132
Bigmore
Armsworth Ho
Wayfarer's Walk
Hill
Northington Down
Fm
Totford
PH
115
Northington
131
Godsfield
Swarraton
Chapel
Lower La
Copse
Newhouse
Swarraton
Fm
Tumuli
The Grange
Fm
Abbotstone
Woods
Lower
Lanham
137
85
Oliver's Battery
Settlement
The Grange
135
Abbotstone
Down
130
98
Nettlebed Fm
Coombe
86
123
35
114
Fm
Itchen Stoke Down
Abbotstone
121
Southdowns
125
Bighton
Manor
Tumuli
66
B 3046
103
Itchen Down
Fm
107
97
34
81
Fobdown Fm
66
Old
Wayfarer's
Alresford
72
Folly Hill
81
Old Alresford
Ho
Pinglestone Fm
Old Alresford
Pond
94
71
111
Bight
Bottom F
Walk
Arlebury
Park
Sch
MS
Gu
33
B 3047
67
Western Court
Itchen
Stoke
55
New
Alresford
Earthwork
58
Bishop's
Sutton
82
PH
MS
Ovington
Tichborne
White
Ovington
Ho
59
Down
Hill
A31
Gospel Oak
102
CH
31
Vernal
Fm
Hampage
Wood
57
Tichborne
Park
Wks
Scrubb
Hampage Fm
Tichborne
Fm
55
56
81
62
Tichborne
Ho
58
59
60
61
PH
Grange Fm
B 3046
Matterley
Fm
Fulley
Wood
Sevington
Fm
112
30
Barley
Down
Ho
101
104
Cheriton
Mill
1644
Field System
North
End
Cheriton Wo
Middle

MAP 16

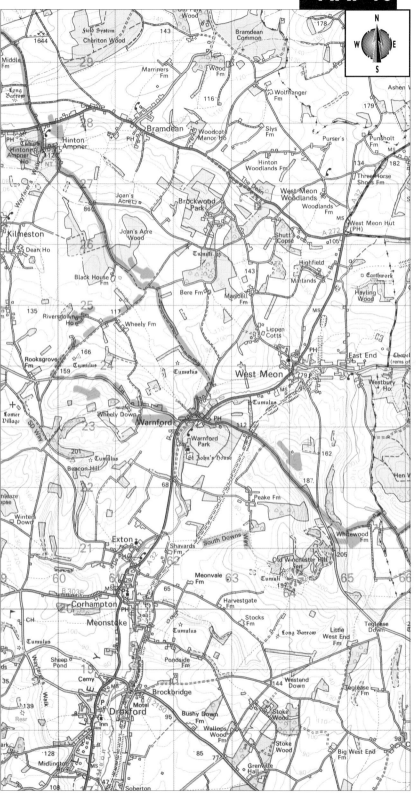

L(ENE), heading for Dummer, 0.8m (1.29km) to the A30. Turn L(NE) (busy road so take care!) 0.2m (322m) to T-junction at the Sun Inn PH then turn R(SE) 0.9m (1.45km) to staggered crossroads in Dummer where you turn R(S) to continue.

DUMMER GRANGE FM

Zigzag R/L, effectively SO(S), on RUPP track 0.5m (805m) to T-junction where metalled surface ends, R(SW) 1m (1.6km), keeping R(SSW) of Dummer Grange, to T-junction by Dummer Grange Farm. Turn L(SE) 0.15m (241m) to T-junction, turn R(WSW) 0.5m (805m), SO(WSW) at Breach Farm T-junction, to T-junction on far side of wood then turn L(S) on tree-lined RUPP (gets muddy when wet) 1.8m (2.9km) to Lone Barn house. Swing L(SSE), through garden alongside house, through gate and 1.1m (1.77km), SO(SE) over Church Lane Farm drive to walk past Brown Candover's church, to the B3046 and there turn R(SW) 0.3m (483km) to T-junction with RUPP track.

BROWN CANDOVER

Turn L(SSE) onto RUPP 0.5m (805m) to T-junction, turn R(SW) then fork L(SSE) at next T-junction to continue SO(SSE) 1.6m (2.57km), with a R/L dogleg at 0.5m (805m), to swing R(SSW) on track crossing just before county classified road at Oliver's Battery car park and picnic site. Go SO(SSW) on county classified road then 1.5m (2.4km), through barrier and continue through woods on obvious singletrack bridleway to track past barn, to Abbotstone Farm crossroads. Turn L(SSW) 0.2m (322m) on to county classified road in Abbotstone **(for Wet Weather Route to New Alresford turn L, see page 69).**

ABBOT-STONE

Turn R(W) over river 0.1m (160m) to crossroads then keep SO(WSW) up RUPP track 0.4m (644m) to staggered crossroads. Turn L(SE) 1.6m (2.57km), SO(SE) county classified road, to T-junction in valley bottom then turn R(S) 0.6m (966m) to county classified road. Turn R(S) 0.4m (644m) to crossroads with the B3047 then turn L(ENE) 0.8m (1.29km) to Broad Street T-junction in the centre of New Alresford.

WET WEATHER ROUTE FROM ABBOTSTONE.
Turn L(E) 2m (3.22km), keep SO at county classified road T-junction, to the B3046 T-junction then turn R(SE) 0.5m (805m) to the top of Broad Street in New Alresford where you turn L(E) to continue.

NEW ALRESFORD

Keep SO(E) 0.1m (160m) down to T-junction, turn R(S) 1m (1.6km), round sharp right bend, to then turn L(S) over footbridge to golf course. Go SO(S then SW) 0.8m (1.29km), across golf course and through woods, to the B3046. Turn L(SSE) 0.1m (160m) and fork L(SE) onto RUPP track 1m (1.6km), keeping L(SE) at track junctions, to crossroads with county classified road. Go SO(SE) 0.9m (1.45km), keeping SO(S) at track junctions, to the A272 crossroads in Hinton Ampner. Go SO(S) 0.4m (644m) on lazy L/R dogleg (where we leave the Wayfarer's Walk for the last time). Turn L(ESE) 0.5m (805m) to crossroads and keep SO(SSE) on unclassified road (tarmac for the first 0.6m – 966m), 1.1m (1.77km) to county classified road. **(For Wet Weather Route avoiding long muddy stretch turn R, see below)**. Turn L(NE) then almost immediately R(ESE) onto unclassified road track 200yds (183m) to T-junction then fork R(S) 0.7m (1.13km) to county classified road where you turn R(SSW) 0.5m (805m), keeping L(SE) at next fork, to A32 in Warnford.

 WET WEATHER ROUTE TO WARNFORD AVOIDING MUDDY UNCLASSIFIED ROAD.
Turn R(SE) 1.5m (2.4km) to crossroads then turn L(E) 1.6m (2.57km) to the A32. Turn L(E) 0.2m (322m) to staggered crossroads in Warnford and there turn R(ESE) to continue.

WARNFORD

Go SO(ESE) 1.7m (2.74km) up Old Winchester Hill to T-junction then keep SO(SE) through gate, onto bridleway (from here to Eastbourne the Wessex Way and South Downs Way share the route where cycling is permitted and it can be

MAP 17

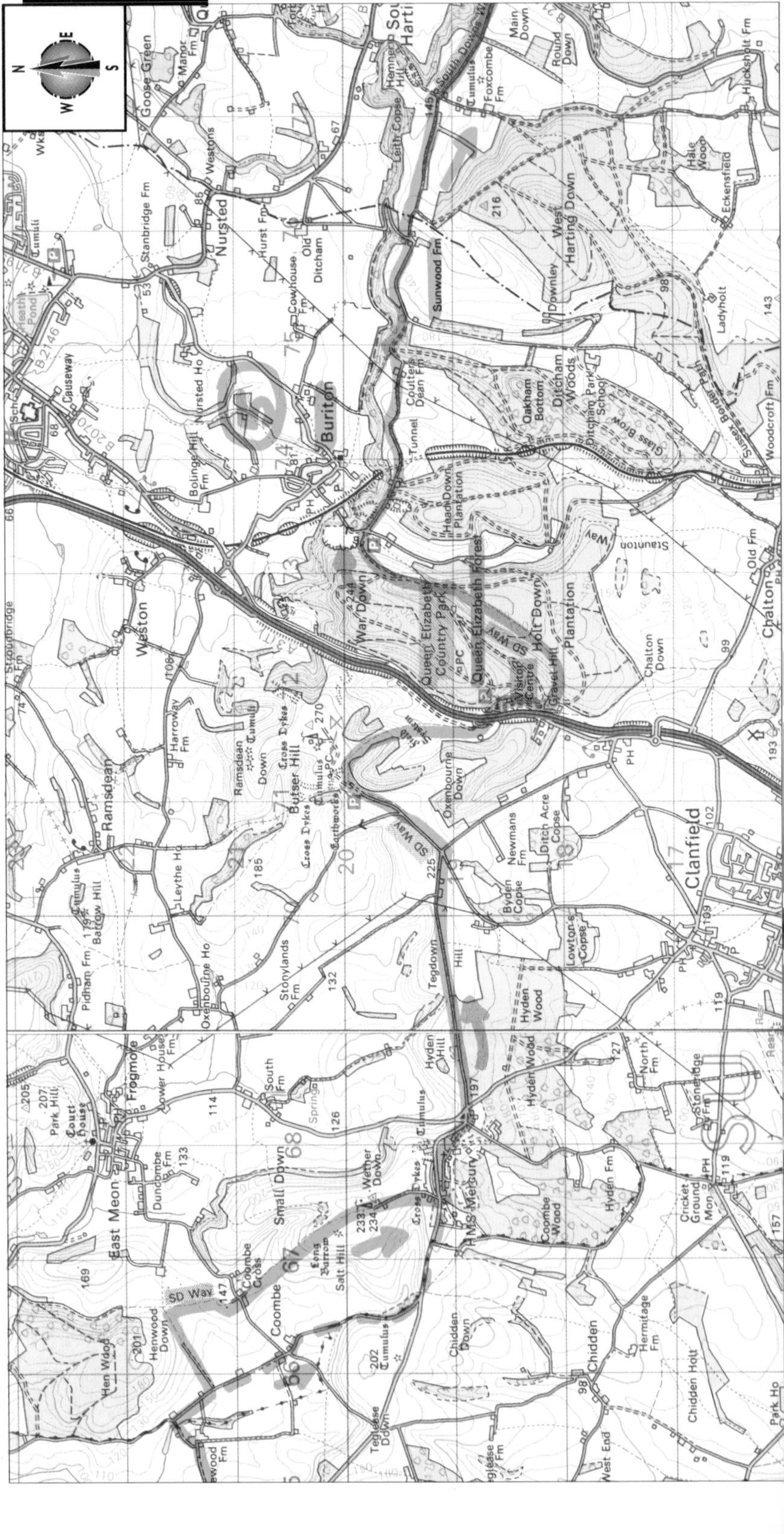

N W E S

Goose Green
Wks
Manor Fm
Weston's
Stanbridge Fm
Nursted
Hurst Fm
Old Ditcham
Cowhouse Fm
Heath Pond
Causeway
B.2146
Bolinge Hill
Nursted Ho
Buriton
Weston
Ramsdean
Harroway Fm
Ramsdean Down
Butser Hill
Cross Dykes
Tumulus
Leythe Ho
Pidham Fm
Bottom Fm
Ovenbourne Ho
Stonylands Fm
Park Hill
Court House
Frogmore
Lower House Fm
South Fm
Duncombe Fm
East Meon
Henwood
Small Down
Coombe Crofts
Salt Hill
SD Way
Coombe
Henwood Downs
Hen Wood
Teglease Down
Teglease Fm

Hemner South
Harti
Leith Copse
Foxcombe
Main Down
Round Down
West Harting Down
Huckholt Fm
Hale Copse
Eckensfield
Downley
Ladyholt
Sunwood Fm
Coulters Dean Fm
Oakham Woods
Ditcham Woods
Ditcham Park School
Glass Brow
Woodcroft
Old Fm
Chalton
Tunnel
Head Down Plantation
Staunton Way
Oxenbourne Down
War Down
Queen Elizabeth Country Park
Queen Elizabeth Forest
Holt Down
Plantation
Chalton Down
PC
Visitor Centre
Gravel Pit
SD Way
Clanfield
Newmans Fm
Ditch Acre Copse
Byden Copse
Lowtons Copse
Hyden Fm
North Fm
Stoneacre
PH
Cricket Ground
Hyden Hill
Hyden Wood
Tegdown Hill
Wether Down
Coombe Wood
HMS Mercury
Cross Dykes
Chidden Down
Chidden
Hermitage Fm
Chidden Holt
Park Fm
Tumulus
West End

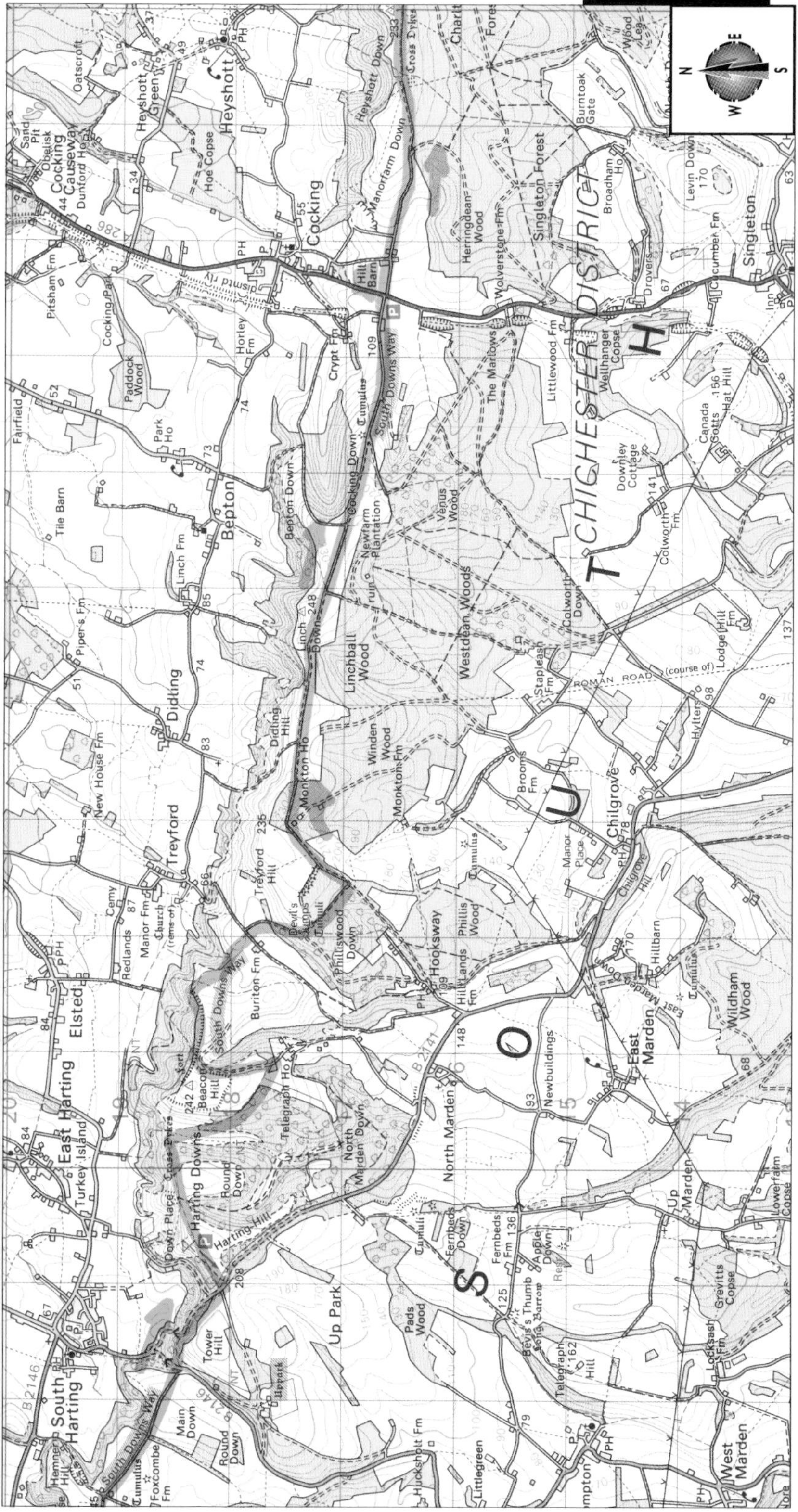

MAP 18

N
E
W
S

Heyshott Green
Heyshott
Sandy
Obelisk
Cocking
Causeway
Dunford Ho
Hoe Copse
Heyshott Down
Cross Dyke
Charlton Forest
Wood Lodge

CHICHESTER DISTRICT

Cocking
Manorfarm Down
Heringdean Wood
Wolverstone Fm
Singleton Forest
Burntoak Gate
Broadham Ho
Levin Down 170
Singleton

Prtsham
Cocking Park
PH
Hill Barn
South Downs Way
The Maltlows
Littlewood Fm
Wellhanger Copse
Canada .156
Hat Hill
Charlton

Fairfield
Paddock Wood
Horley Fm
Crypt Fm
109
Cumulus
Downley Cottage
141
Chilcumber Fm
Drovers

Tile Barn
Park Ho
Bepton Down
Cocking Down
Venus Wood
Colworth Down
Colworth Fm
90
Lodge Hill Fm
137

Piper's Fm
Didling
New House Fm
Lunch Fm
85
Linch Down 248
Linchball Wood
Westdean Woods
Staple Ash
Fm
ROMAN ROAD (course of)
Hylter

Treyford
Didling Hill
Monkton Ho
Winden Wood
Monkton Down
Broons Fm
Chilgrove
PH 78
Manor Place

Manor Fm
Church
Redlands
Treyford Hill
Devil's Jumps
Phillswood
Down
Phillis Wood
Hooksway
Chilgrove Hill
Hilltbarn
East Marden
Wildham Wood

Elsted
Buriton Fm
Hookslands
Fm
Newbuildings

East Harting
Turkey Island
Beacon
Hill
Telegraph Ho
North Marden Down
North Marden
93
Up Marden

South Harting
Harting Down
Round Down Hill
Harting Hill
Up Park
Pads Wood
Fernbeds Down
Fernbeds Fm 136
Apple Down
Devil's Thumb
Long Barrow
Telegraph Hill
Cocksnap Grevitts Copse

B2146
Hemner Hill
Main Down
Round Down Fm
Huckshlt Fm
Littlegreen
West Marden

busy with walkers and horses at times so please take extra care. Waymarking on this National Trail is excellent). Continue 0.8m (1.29km) (watch out for the gate at 0.4m (644m) and sharp chicane down by the farm!) to county classified road then turn R(SE) 0.25m (402m) to T-junction. **(For Wet Weather Route, avoiding mud and slippery Salt Hill climb to HMS Mercury keep SO, see below)** Turn L(ENE) on bridleway track 0.5m (805m) over hill to crossroads, turn R(S) 1.8m (2.9km), over county classified road at Combe Cross and up Salt Hill, to county classified road at HMS Mercury.

WET WEATHER ROUTE TO HMS MERCURY.
Keep SO(SSE) 1.7m (2.74km), through Combe and up hill, to RUPP/county classified road crossroads then turn L(ESE) 0.5m (805m) to RUPP/county classified road staggered crossroads just as you get to HMS Mercury. Keep SO(E) to continue.

HMS MERCURY

Turn L(E) 0.6m (966m), SO(E) at next crossroads, to crossroads with RUPP track and go SO(E) 1.5m (2.4km) to crossroads. Turn L(NE), heading for Butser Hill, 0.7m (1.13km) where, just before the entrance to Butser Hill recreation area, you fork R(NE) on singletrack bridleway that swings round R(E) 125yds (114m) to bridle-gate. Swing R(SE then S) through gate 1m (1.6km) down (watch out for bridle-gate at 0.5m – 805m!) steep grass hill then past Butser Hill Iron Age Hill Farm project and under the A3 into the Queen Elizabeth Country Park Visitor Centre.

QUEEN ELIZABETH COUNTRY PARK

For off-road route avoiding Visitor Centre follow waymarker emblazoned with blue horseshoe. Fork L(SE), just after passing beneath the A3, up onto singletrack bridleway for 0.6m (966m) that circles south round the Centre. Swing R(W) across car parks, fork L(S) and after a few yards turn L(E) across the southern end of the Centre back onto singletrack for steep climb up to forest fire road. Turn R(S) 20yds (18m) up hill then turn L(SE then

E) onto singletrack bridleway 1.7m (2.74km), up over forested hill, to crossroads with county classified road (watch out for the gate just before the road!). **(Suggested overnight stop)**

DAY 6 Maps 17 – 21

BURITON TO UPPER BEEDING/TRULEIGH HILL YHA
41 miles (66 km) (35 miles (56 km) off-road) Summits: Beacon Hill – 242m; Heyshott Down – 233m; Bignor Hill – 225m; Rackham Hill – 193m; Chanctonbury Ring – 236m.

Of the two days spent spinning along the undulating South Downs section of the Wessex Way this one is the easiest. Granny-cog slogs there are a few but for the most part you'll have a ridge top cruise when those steaming calves can simmer down. Then it's prime-time gravity pull to pump up the adrenaline factor. In summer the water points along the way come in handy and there's a highly convenient bike shop in Storrington. Get there by dropping north on waymarked bridleway 0.5m (800m) after the barn on Sullington Hill and return to the Way via Washington. Once you've dropped down into the Adur valley keep going north up the A283 then take the A2037 into Upper Beeding. Alternatively, if you can handle another climb, carry on to Truleigh Hill and take in a YHA overnight.

Go SO(ESE) 0.75m (1.21km), on tarmac at first then on track (slippery in the wet!), to T-junction then turn R(SE) 0.7m (1.13km), through Coulters Farm then swing L(NNE) and – on tarmac – swing R(ESE) to T-junction. Turn L(ENE) 0.5m (805m) to Sunwood Farm.

SUNWOOD FARM Fork R(E) onto RUPP track 1.6m (2.57km), going SO(E) at T-junction and crossroads with bridleway, to the B2146 (busy road so take care crossing!). Go SO(E) for singletrack climb 0.5m (805m) to join county classified road to Harting Hill car park and picnic site. Turn L(ENE) over grass then chalk track to north of the site 1m (1.6km) to bridleway crossroads (turn left to

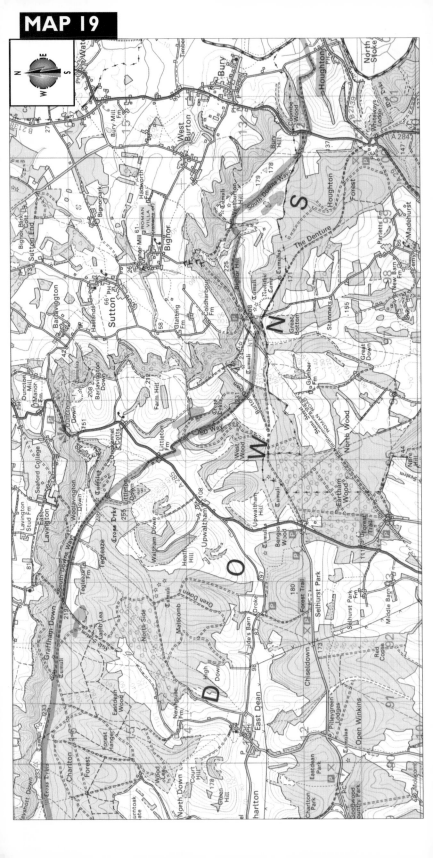

MAP 19

MAP 20

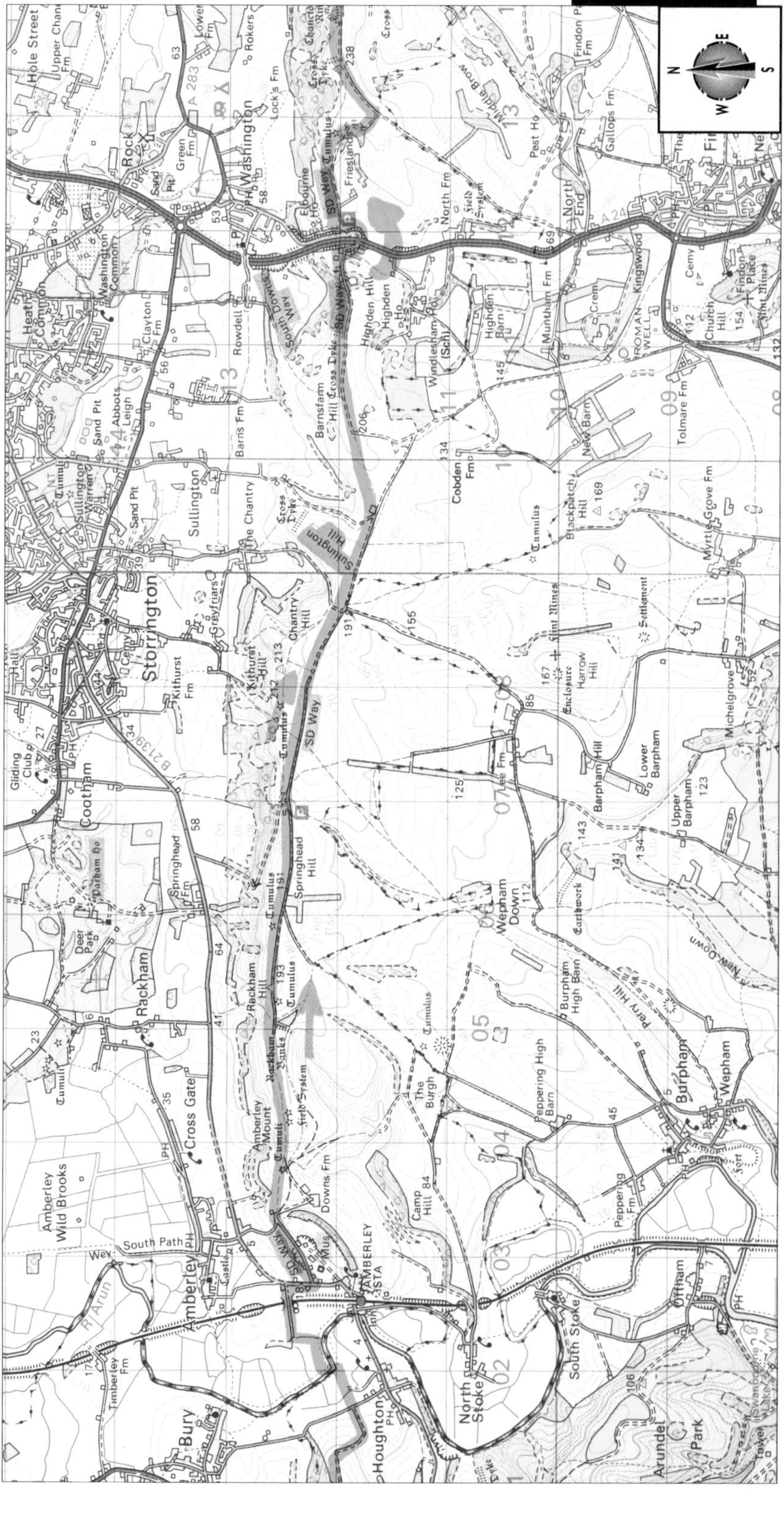

N
W E
S

Hole Street
Upper Channel
Lower Channel
Rokers Hill
Rokers Fm
Cross
Middle Brow
138
Pest Ho
Findon Place
Gallops Fm
Rock
Green Fm
Sand Pit
63
A 283
Church Hill
Locks Fm
Cross
North Fm
North End
A 24
Findon
Findon Place
Flint Mines
Washington
58
53
Elbourne
Freeland
North Fm
swb
swb
system
A 24
Muntham Fm
Kingswood
ROMAN WELL
Cemy
Chichester Hill
Findon
Place
112
154
Heath Common
Washington Common
Clayton Fm
56
Rowdell
Highden Hill
Highden
Highden Hill
Highden Barn
Wordlesham (Sch)
145
New Barn
Tolmare Fm
152
Sand Pit
Abbots Leigh
Baris Fm
Barnsham Fm
South Dro
Hill Cross Dyke Tumulus
SD Way
206
Cobden Fm
134
Tumulus
Blackpatch Hill
169
Myrtle Grove Fm
Sullington Warren NT
Sand Pit
Sullington
The Chantry
Cross Dyke
Sullington Hill
Flint Mines
167
Enclosure
85
Harrow Hill
Settlement
Storrington
Grey Friars
Chantry Hill
191
155
168
Lee Fm
Barpham Hill
Lower Barpham
Upper Barpham
Michelgrove
123
Kithurst Fm
Kithurst Hill
213
Tumulus
SD Way
125
143
141
134
New Down
Gliding Club
27
Cootham
58
Springhead
Springhead Hill
191
Tumulus
Wepham Down
112
Earthwork
Perry Hill
Deer Pk
Parham Pk
64
Rackham
Rackham Hill
Tumulus
193
Tumulus
Burpham High Barn
Burpham
Wepham
23
Tumulus
35
Cross Gate
41
Rackham Bank
Field System
The Burgh
Peppering High Barn
45
Amberley Mount
Tumuli
Amberley Wild Brooks
South Path
Wey
R Arun
Amberley
Downs Fm
Camp Hill 84
04
03
Peppering Fm
Burpham
Castle
AMBERLEY STA
North Stoke
02
South Stoke
Offham
106
Timberley Fm
Bury
Houghton
Arundel Park

descend to East Harting and Oakwood B & B). Turn R(S) 0.75m (1.21km) to T-junction then L(NNW) 0.5m (805m) down to crossroads then go SO(ESE) 0.5m (805m), straight over Pen Hill (sharp right bend on far side!) to crossroads with RUPP. Go SO(ESE then S) on singletrack bridleway (muddy in the wet) 0.5m (805m), joining grassy track, to staggered crossroads where you zigzag L/R to climb 0.75m (1.21km), keep L(SSE) at bridleway fork, to crossroads with footpath and RUPP. Turn L(NE) 3.5m (5.63km), keeping SO(E and ESE) at junctions, for roller-coaster ridge run then descent to the A286 below Hill Barn.

HILL BARN
Go SO(E) going SO junctions 4.5m (7.24km), through Hill Barn (water tap here during the summer), on obvious SDW track emerging into field on Littleton Down. Go SO(SE) 0.5m (805m), on singletrack bridleway and through bridle-gate, to join track and keep SO(SSE) (farmer strings barbed wire across tracks here so be careful!) 0.1m (160m) down to A285 crossroads at Littleton Farm. Go SO(SSE) (gets gruesomely muddy just here) 2m (3.22km), up through z-bend to keep R(SSE) at fork that follows and SO(E) at crossroads to go alongside field boundary south of the radio masts, to crossroads. Turn L(NE then E) 0.25m (402m) to crossroads and car park with a Latin signpost below and before Bignor Hill.

BIGNOR HILL
Keep SO(ENE), passing the end of the county classified road then past the bridle-gate, 1m (1.6km) over Bignor Hill and through gate to T-junction with waymarker. Turn L(NNE) 0.2m (322m) down to staggered crossroads then zigzag L/R, effectively SO(E) past the barns (muddy when wet here) 1.1m (1.77km) to complex crossroads (to go to Whiteways Picnic Site and R & R facilities fork right and follow bridleway SSE 0.75m (1.21km) then return N along the A284 to continue). Follow SDW waymarker and keep SO(ESE) 0.2m (322m) to staggered crossroads with the A284 then zigzag R/L 50yds (46m), effectively SO(E) 1m (1.6km) (sharp R/L chicane at 0.5m – 805m!) to crossroads with county classified road near Houghton.

MAP 20-21

HOUGHTON

Go SO(ENE) 1m (1.6km), on obvious gated track over bridleway bridge over River Arun then through gate, away from river, to the B2139. Turn R(S) 0.15m (241m), keeping to obvious path and crossing road, to T-junction then turn L(ENE) 0.5m (805m), swing R(E) at county classified road T-junction ahead, to T-junction with bridleway track. Turn L(ESE) up very steep bridleway, 0.2m (322m) to gated track (muddy here when wet) then keep L(E) over steep hill and then along ridge top, keeping SO(E) at junctions 3.7m (5.95km) to fork at barn on Sullington Hill.

SULLINGTON HILL

Keep L(E) alongside fence at first 1.7m (2.74km), SO(E) at junctions, to crossroads with A24 (extremely fast and busy road! Take care crossing. There's also a water tap on the last bend as you approach the main road). Go SO(E then immediately N) 150yds (137m) to T-junction then turn R(E) 0.9m (1.45km), keeping R(ESE) at fork at 0.3m (483km), to T-junction. Turn L(NE) 3m (4.83km), passing Chanctonbury Ring fort then SO junctions, to join county classified road above Steyning Bowl – a valley head. Turn R(S) 0.6m (966m) to bridleway T-junction then turn L(E) on singletrack bridleway across fields, alongside fence at first then keep to the top of the spur 1.4m (2.25km) with a fast descent to a gate. Keep L(E) through gate 0.4m (644m) (sharp left bend!) to county classified road then turn R(E) 0.5m (805m) to T-junction with bridleway track and there turn L(E) through gate 0.3m (483m), over River Adur on Botolphs bridge (water tap here, behind trough).

OFF-ROAD CODE
- **Do not race**
- **Keep erosion to a minimum and do not skid**

MAP 21

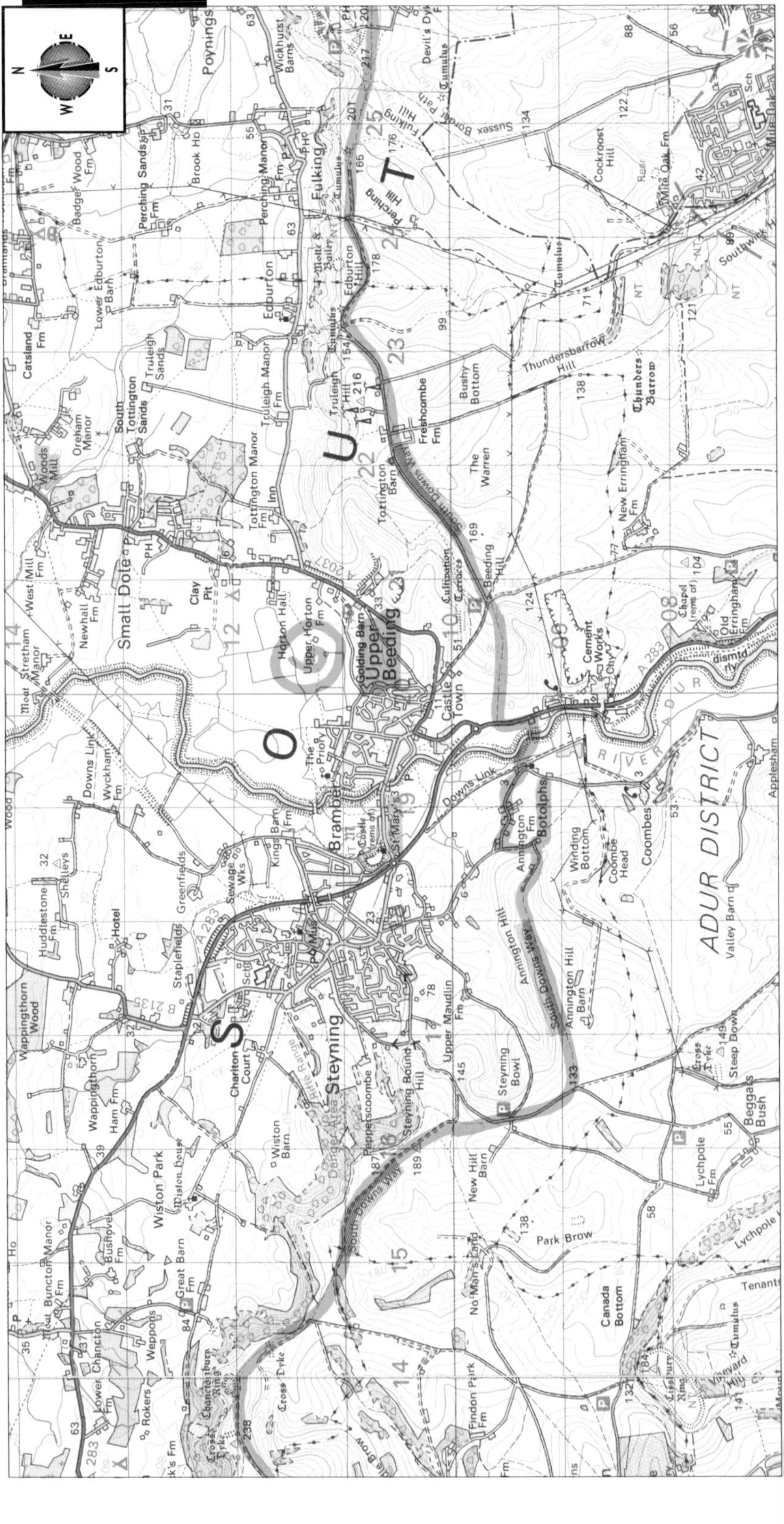

N E W S

Poynings
Wickhurst Barns
Devil's Dyke
Sch
Badger's Wood Fm
Perching Sands Fm
Brook Ho
Perching Manor Fm
Fulking
Perching Hill
Sussex Border Path
Fulking Hill
Cockroost Hill
Wild Oak Fm
Southw
Lower Edburton Barn
Catsland Fm
Edburton Sands
Nestr's Hostry
Edburton
Truleigh Sands
Truleigh Manor Fm
Truleigh Hill
Freshcombe Fm
Thundersbarrow Hill
Thundersbarrow
Bushy Bottom
New Erringham Fm
Orehan Manor
South Tottington Sands
Tottington Manor
Tottington Inn
Tottington Barn
The Warren
Beeding Hill
Cement Works
Old Erringham Fm
Chapel (rems of)
Woods Mill
Moat
Stretham Manor
Newhall Fm
West Mill Fm
Small Dole
Clay Pit
Horton Hall
Upper Horton Fm
Golding Barn
Cultivation Terraces
Castle Town
Upper Beeding
Cement Works
dismtd rly
Wyckham Fm
Shelleys
Downs Link
The Priory
Bramber
Castle (rems of)
St Mary's (M)
Kings Barn Fm
Botolphs
Annington Hill
Coombes
Appleshaw
RIVER ADUR
ADUR DISTRICT
Huddlestone Fm
Hotel
Staplefield
Greenfields
Sewage Wks
Annington Fm
Annington Hill
Annington Hill Barn
Winding Bottom
Coombe Head
Coombes
Valley Barn
Wappingthorn Wood
Wappingthorn Manor
Wappingthorn Ham Fm
Charlton Court
Newham Fm
Steyning
South Downs Way
Upper Maudlin
Steyning Bowl
Steyning Round Hill
Steyning Bowl
Cross Dyke
Steep Down
Beggars Bush
Lychpole Fm
Wiston Park
Wiston Barn
Wiston House
Pepperscoombe
New Hill Barn
Park Brow
Lychpole
Ho
Mouse Buncton Manor
Bushovel Fm
Great Barn Fm
Lower Chancton Fm
Weppots
No Man's Land
Findon Park Fm
Canada Bottom
Vineyard
Tenant
Chanctonbury Ring
Cross Dyke
Ks Fm

MAP 22

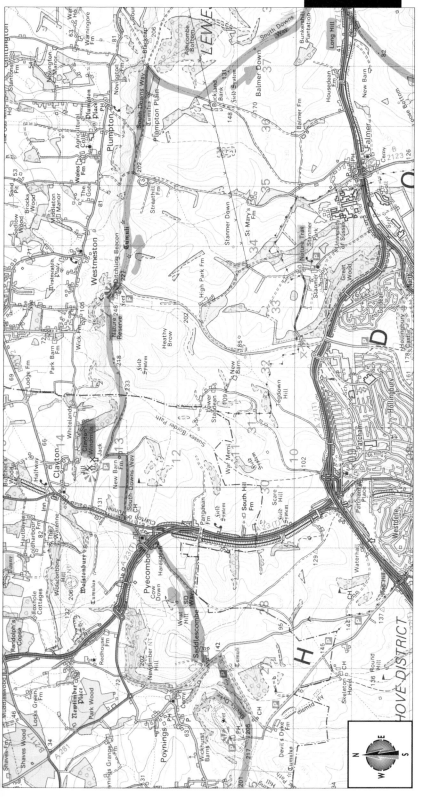

BOTOLPHS
Turn L(N) alongside A283 0.1m (160m) to T-junction with bridleway. Turn R(E), crossing road, 0.7m (1.13km) up to crossroads with county classified road then keep SO(ENE) on tarmac at first 1m (1.6km) to Truleigh Hill YHA (there's water here). Keep SO(ENE) on obvious track 2.4m (3.86km), roughly following escarpment edge, to bridle-gate.**(Suggested overnight stop)**

DAY 7 Maps 21 – 25

UPPER BEEDING TO ALFRISTON
**29 miles (47 km) (25.5 miles (41 km) off-road)
Summits: Truleigh Hill – 216m; Ditchling Beacon – 248m; Swanborough Hill – 192m; Iford Hill – 164m.**

If you're feeling super fit and you've overnighted at Truleigh Hill you could finish the ride today. And die! If you were a bit disappointed with the lack of vista fixes yesterday then today, weather permitting, you'll be treated to quite a few. Our route keeps to the escarpment edge for much of the time with wide views over the Weald and rolling scenery down to the sea. Can be quite aerial on a clear day! There's some nifty single-track down into Saddlescombe but the grass climb out's a...! Well it is if you're tired! Don't forget to take a look at the Jack and Jill windmills and to turn right off Plumpton Plain. Then it's Intercity trailblazing, over the A27 and some exhausting hill hopping over to Alfriston. If Telscombe YHA grabs your fancy hang an off-road right 0.3m (480m) after the Rodmell turn.

SADDLES-COMBE
Keep SO(ENE) on obvious track 2.4m (3.86km), roughly following escarpment edge, to bridle-gate. Over to your L is Devil's Dyke Hotel on the escarpment edge. Go SO(E) through gate across rough pasture on bridleway singletrack 0.4m (644m) to county classified road. Go SO(E then ENE) on narrow bridleway track, between escarpment edge to the north and a county classified road 100yds (91m) south, 1.1m (1.77km) down to crossroads with county classified road at Saddlescombe. Go SO(NE then E) 0.8m (1.29km),

MAP 22

through hamlet and through gate, up over West Hill to crossroads then keep L(NE) 0.7m (1.13km) down to the old A23. Turn L(NW) 0.2m (322m) then turn R(NE) over the new A23 then immediately turn R(ESE) 0.25m (402m), through hamlet, to the A273. Turn L(NNE) 200yds (183m) to T-junction turn R(E) 0.75m (1.21km), past golf course, to crossroads then turn L(N) 0.25m

CLAYTON WINDMILLS (402m) to crossroads close by Clayton Windmills (worth a very short detour for the view).

Turn R(ESE) on obvious ridge top track 2m (3.22km), SO junctions, to crossroads with county classified road then keep SO(ESE), again on ridge top track and SO(ESE) crossroads with unclassified road, 2.5m (4.02km) to crossroads (easy to go straight through). Turn R(SW) away from escarpment edge 0.75m (1.21km) to T-junction then turn L(SE) and following field boundaries 1.5m (2.4km) down to valley bottom. Go through gate then swing R(SSE), on grass singletrack at first, 0.25m (402m) passing through wood to gate. Go through gate and swing R(SW) 0.25m (402m) down to staggered crossroads with the bridleway and the A27 below Long Hill.

OFF-ROAD CODE
● **Be courteous and considerate to others**
● **Be self-sufficient and make sure your bike is safe to ride**

MAP 23

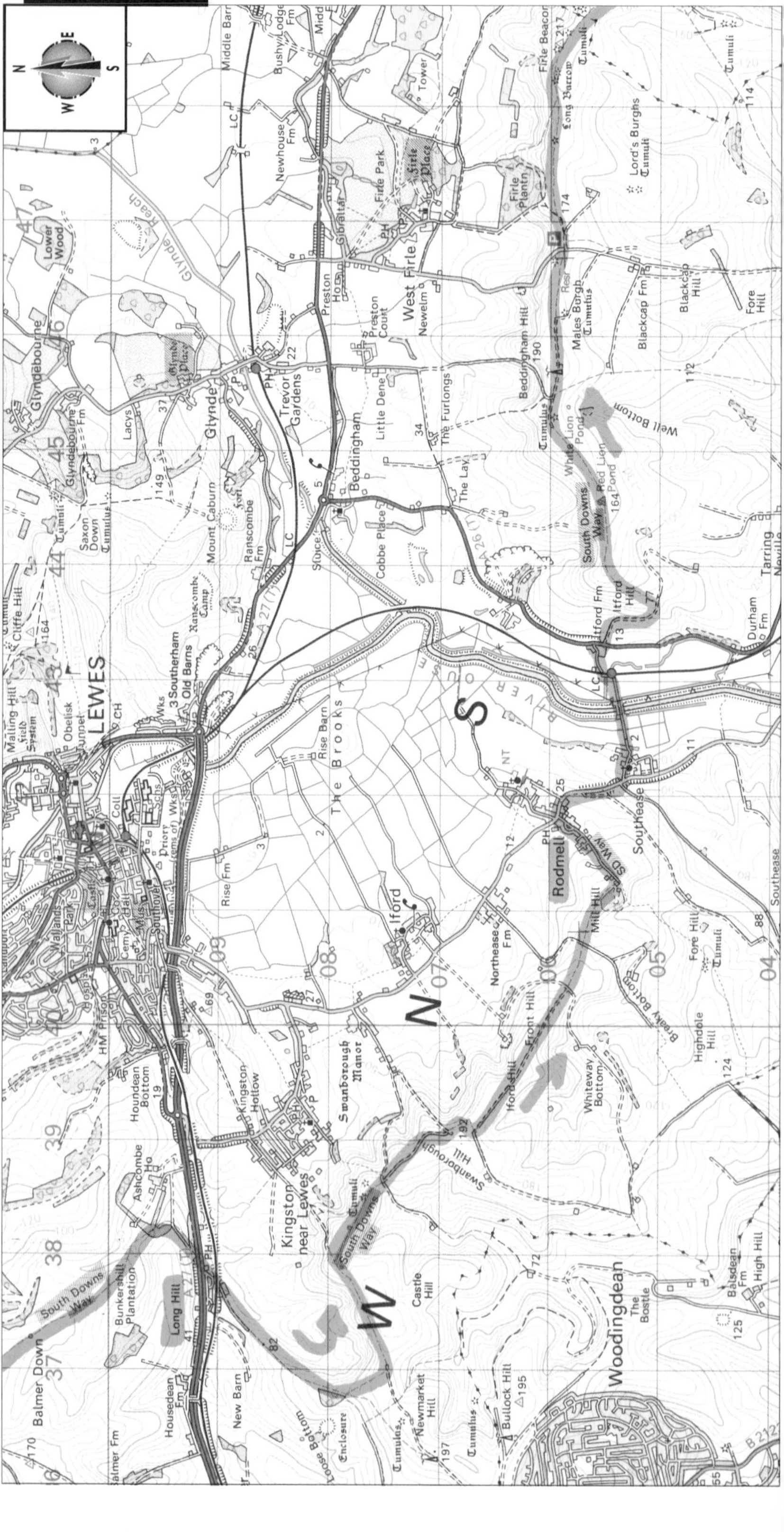

LEWES
Malling Hill
Obelisk
Tunnel
Cliffe Hill
Southerham
Old Barns
Ranscombe Camp
Mount Caburn
Ranscombe Fm
Saxon Down
Glyndebourne
Glyndebourne Fm
Lower Wood
Glynde
Glynde Place
Glynde Reach
Lacys
Trevor Gardens
Newhouse Fm
Bushy Lodge Fm
Middle Barn
Preston Ho
Preston Court
Gibraltar
Firle Park
Firle Place
Firle Plantn
West Firle
Newelm
Tower
Firle Beacon
Long Barrow
Lord's Burghs
Beddingham
Beddingham Hill
Little Dene
The Furlongs
The Lay
Cobbe Place
Sluice
Males Burgh
Blackcap Fm
Blackcap Hill
Fore Hill
Well Bottom
White Lion Pond
Red Lion Pond
South Downs Way
Itford Fm
Itford Hill
Durham Fm
Tarring Neville
RIVER OUSE
The Brooks
Rise Barn
Rise Fm
Iford
Rodmell
Southease
Northease Fm
Mill Hill
SD Way
Front Hill
Iford Hill
Whiteway Bottom
Breaky Bottom
Highdole Hill
Fore Hill
Swanborough Manor
Swanborough Hill
Kingston Hollow
Kingston near Lewes
Priory (rems of)
Southover
HM Prison
Houndean Bottom
Ashcombe Ho
Castle Hill
Woodingdean
The Bostle
Balsdean Fm
High Hill
Bullock Hill
Newmarket Hill
Enclosure
Loose Bottom
New Barn
Housedean Fm
Long Hill
Bunkershill Plantation
Balmer Down
Balmer Fm
Tumuli
Tumulus
N
S
W
E

MAP 24

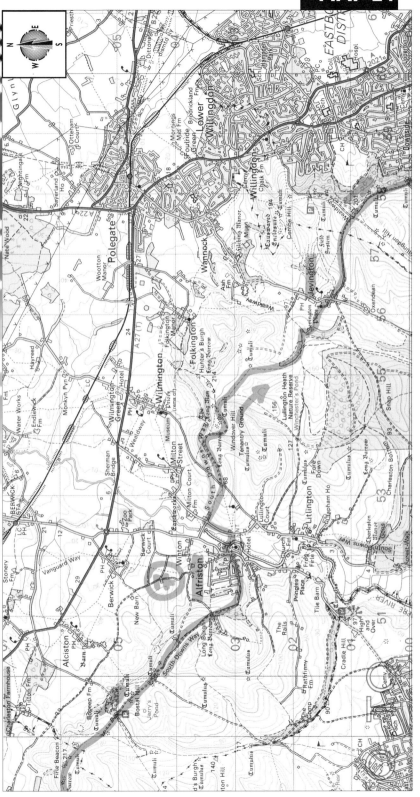

MAP 23

LONG HILL/A27

Zigzag R/L to cross the A27 (extremely busy road so take care!), effectively SO(SE) past PH and under rail bridge then keep R(SE) 1.25m (2.01km) up bridleway track to T-junction by copse. Swing L(SSE) through gate 0.25m (402m) to T-junction, swing L(ENE) 0.75m (1.21km) to fork then swing R(ESE) on singletrack bridleway over grass 0.5m (805m) to crossroads. Keep SO(SE) along escarpment edge 0.6m (966m) to zigzag R/L then, on metalled bridleway, continue (SE) 1.75m (2.82km) going SO(SE) junctions to T-junction at Mill Hill then turn L(NE) 0.5m (805m) down to staggered crossroads with county classified road in Rodmell.

RODMELL

Turn R(ESE) 0.5m (805m) to staggered crossroads then turn L(ESE) 1m (1.6km), beside Southease green then on over River Ouse and past the BR station, to staggered crossroads with the A26 at Itford Farm (there's a water tap in the yard for SDW users). Zigzag R/L, effectively SO(ESE), onto bridleway track 0.5m (805m) to fork then keep L(NE), onto singletrack bridleway over grass at first, 2.25m (3.62km) past radio mast to crossroads with county classified road off north. Keep SO(E) 3.3m (5.31km), passing trig point on Firle Beacon then keeping SO(SE) at junctions, down to tricky crossroads. Here you effectively keep SO(SSE) 1m (1.6km), swing L(E) at 0.3m (483km), down into Alfriston. **(Suggested overnight stop)**

OFF-ROAD CODE
- **Wear a helmet**
- **Follow a route marked on a map**

MAP 24

DAY 8 Maps 24 – 25

ALFRISTON TO BEACHY HEAD
**12 miles (19 km) (9.2 miles (15 km) off-road)
Summits: Windover Hill – 214m; Willingdon
Hill – 201m.**

It's scenic saunter day. The last leg and you can afford to take things a bit easy with just two big climbs and a sweet descent sandwiched between. Don't wander up on to the top of Wilmington Hill – if you pass the trig then you know you've overshot. On the fly down to Jevington remember to hang a right and pick up the single-track otherwise you'll miss out on some excellent riding. We were enveloped in mist which meant we didn't see the sea until we stopped at the cliff-top. I hope you fare better because the end is dramatic. The Wessex Way just wings into space with the sea 350ft below! Now go and celebrate in the pub up the road – you've just completed the longest coast-to-coast ride in England!

ALFRISTON Turn L(N) 25yds (23m), past the Star Inn, then R(E) just before road island 100yds (91m) down lane to Cuckmere River bank. Turn R(S) 25yds (23m) then turn L(E) 200yds (183m), over bridge, to county classified road then turn L(N) 0.25m (402m) to crossroads with RUPP. Turn R(ESE) 0.5m (805m) up to county classified road. Go SO(ENE) 1m (1.6km) on old coach road that describes a lazy reverse 'S' as it climbs to bridle-gate. Go through gate and swing R(SE) on faint singletrack bridleway over grass (posts guide you but do not swing further R(SSW) on grass track down Tenantry spur) 1.25m (2.01km) eventually swinging R(S) down to crossroads. Keep L(E) for 0.2m (322m) then fork R(SE) onto singletrack then bridleway track 0.5m (805m), past church, to county classified road in Jevington.

JEVINGTON Turn R(S) 50yds (46m) then turn L(ESE) up bridleway track 2.7m (4.35km), keeping SO through junctions on obvious track that swings slowly south, to crossroads with county classified road by the golf course club house. Go SO(SSE) for 0.25m (402m) to fork then keep R(SSE) (here

MAP 25

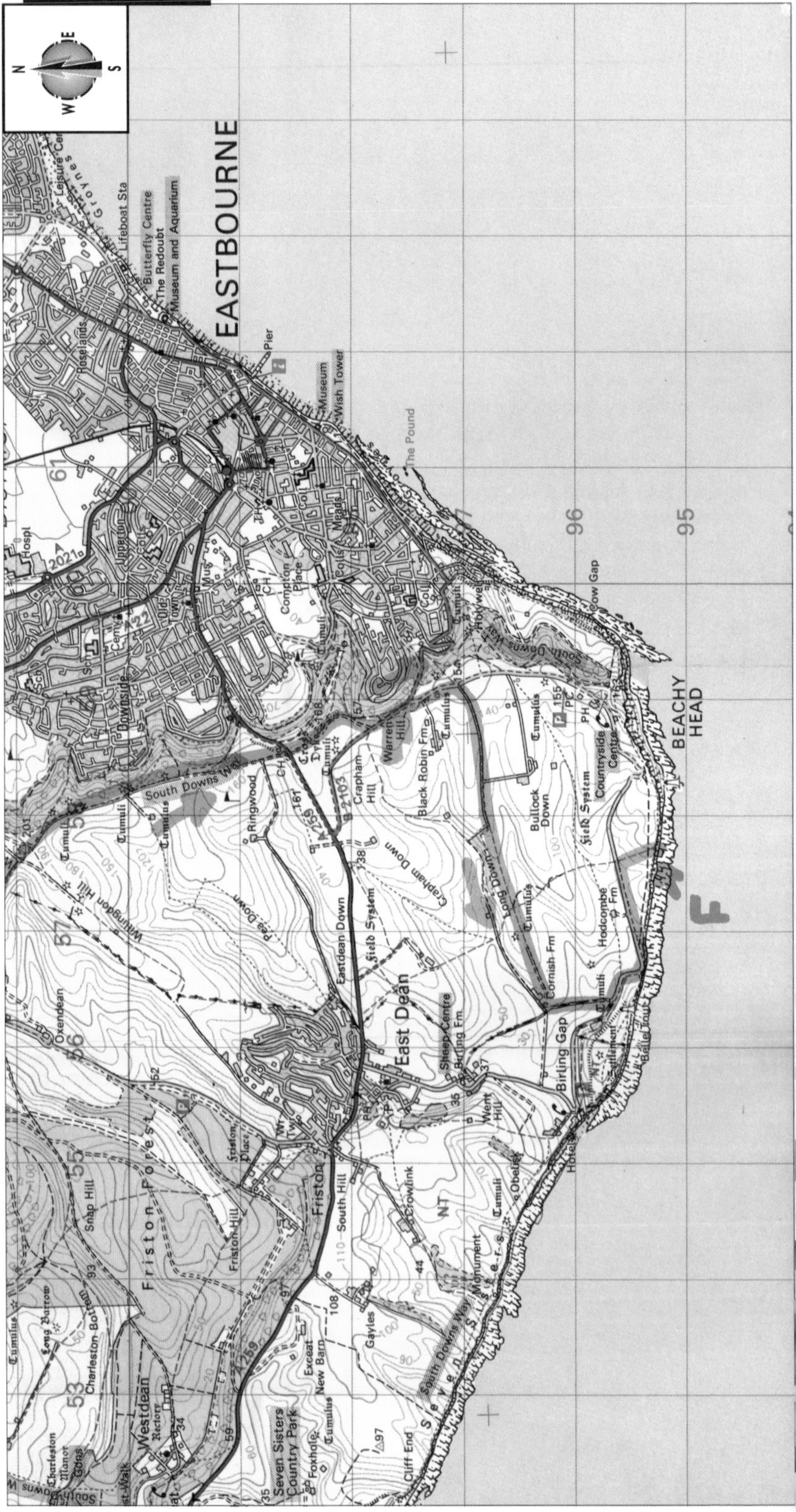

N E W S

EASTBOURNE

Leisure Cen
Lifeboat Sta
Butterfly Centre
The Redoubt
Museum and Aquarium
Pier
Wish Tower
Museum

Hosp

Compton
Park

The Pound

Col

South Downs Way

Low Gap

BEACHY
HEAD

Warren Hill
Tumulus
PC
PH
P

Crapham
Hill

Black Robin Fm

Bullock
Down

Ringwood

Field System

Field System

Crapham Down

Long Down

Eastdean Down

Hodcombe
Fm

Cornish Fm

Pea Down

Willingdon Hill

Cornish
Fm

Oxendean

Tumuli

East Dean

Sheep Centre
Birling Fm

Birling Gap

Friston Forest

Friston

Snap Hill

Friston
Place

Went
Hill

Charleston Bottom

South Hill

Fristoh Hill

Crowlink

NT

Tumuli

Obelisk

Long Barrow

Foxhole
Exceat
New Barn

Gayles

Monument

South Downs Way

Westdean
Rectory

Seven Sisters
Country Park

Cliff End

Charleston Manor

South Downs Way

MAP 25

we leave the South Downs Way and keep to the west of the trig and dew pond) 0.25m (402m) swing R(SW) to the B2103 at Warren Hill.

WARREN HILL Turn L(SSE) for 0.3m (483km) to T-junction then fork R(SSE) 0.3m (483km) to crossroads with bridleway and there turn R(WSW) 2m (3.22km) then L(S) at Cornish Farm 0.3m (483km) to county classified road. Turn L(ESE) 0.9m (1.45km) to crossroads with bridleway then turn R(SSE) for final 0.25m (402m) climb on grass to the edge of the 330ft high chalk cliffs of Beachy Head.

BEACHY HEAD Pose for photos then return to county classified road, turn R(ENE) 1m (1.6km) to the Beachy Head PH for a well-deserved bevy!

DAY RIDES ON THE WESSEX WAY

The following three day rides are all circular tours which can either be added to the main route, or completed as separate tours in themselves. The maps for these day rides follow in the next few pages.

South Downs Loop [MAP A]

Distance: 17 miles (27 km)
Time: 2 hours (3 hours when wet)
A dip-and-dive ride that packs in a bit of everything. Hard-pack trail, tortuous single-track with some sliding between the trees plus a couple of leg-busting climbs. A bit of a traction teaser in the wet but fast and furious on a dry day.

LOCATION | ROUTE DIRECTIONS

STANE STREET CAR PARK Start from 'Stane Street' car park above Bignor (GR974129). Head west, towards the radio masts, for 150yds (137m) to crossroads. SO(WNW) for 1m (1.6km), passing masts, down rutted track to bridleway path off R. Keep (NNE not ENE) then L(N) across valley, over Farm Hill to crossroads 0.9m (1.45km) away. SO(N) alongside wood, over

A285

Barlavington Down as track swings L(NW) then R(NE) down into woods and crossroads 0.7m (1.13km) away. L(WNW) for 200yds (183m), hairpin R and follow zigzag track down to A285 400yds (366m) away.

Turn R(N). Road sweeps L. Go SO(W) on to Beechwood Lane (dead end). After 0.9m (1.45m) bridleway track starts gentle, westerly roller coaster for 1m (1.6km) (ignore L forks uphill) to multiple crossroads. L then keep R(SW) and climb 0.5m (805m) up Graffham Down to crossroads on South Downs Way (SDW). Keep SO(SW) 2.6m (4.18km), joining track in valley bottom at 1m

EAST DEAN

(1.6km), to T-junction just past East Dean church. Turn R(WSW) for 1.25m (2.01km), after keeping SO(SW) at T-junction in the village, up to crossroads. Turn L(E) on tarmac for 0.5m (805m) to woods, pick up parallel track on L for 1m then

DROKE

L(N) on bridleway track down to Droke. L(NNW) on road, 75yds (69m), R(N) through gate and up track, single-track and track heading N/NNE for 1m climb to T-junction. L(N) on main track, 500yds (457m) to crossroads. 1st R(E) on grassy track, out of forest, along its edge then cross field to SDW 1.5m (2.4km) away. R(SE) on signed

LITTLETON FARM

SDW for 2.5m (4.02km), past Littleton Farm on A285, to bridleway crossroads at Burton Down. L(NE) towards masts. 0.4m (644m) R(SE) at T-junction (now back on outbound trail) for 0.6m (966m) to start.

Salisbury Plain Loop [MAP B]

Distance: 16 miles (26 km)
Time: 2.5 hours
Not the Plain's usual fare of broad tracks and rolling hills but a bagatelle of bridleways and RUPPS with demonic descents and scintillating single-track to quicken the pulse.

COLLING- BOURNE KINGSTON

Start at Cleaver Inn (GR239559). L(N) 100yds (91m) then R(NE) 1m (1.6km) through Brunton then R(ESE) at Spicey Buildings barn. 1m (1.6km),

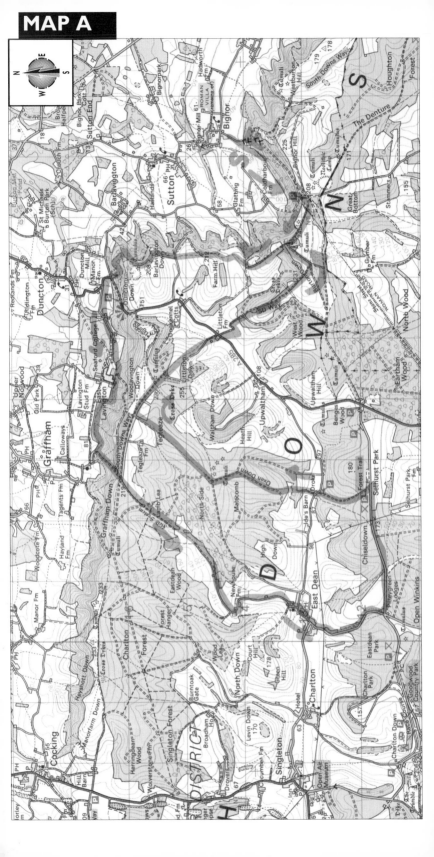

MAP A

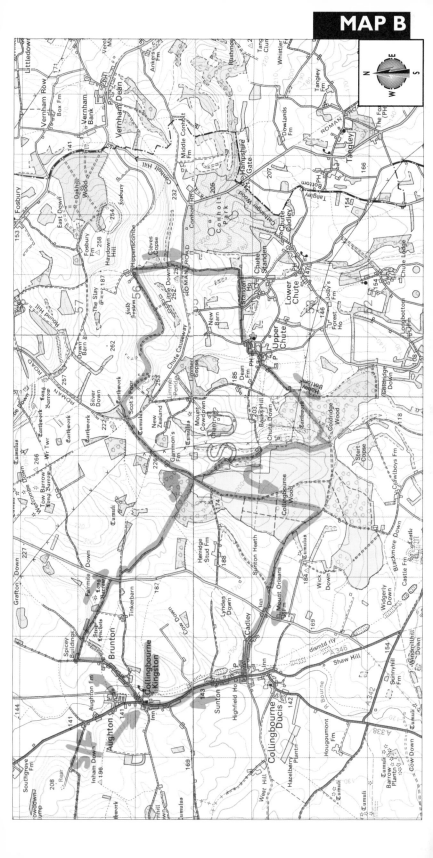

keeping SO(ESE) at T-junction, to road then R(S) 200yds (183m), L(E) on track 80yds (73m) to T-junction, R(SE) 1.3m (2.09km), across valley and through woods, to track T-junction beyond field.

SCOT'S POOR

L(NE) 1.1m (1.77km) to Scot's Poor then go SO(E) onto single-track bridleway hard by L(N) side of cottage 2m (3.22km) along meandering valley bottom to Hippenscombe Farm T-junction. R(S) 1.25m (2.01km) over Little Down, SO(S) road, to RUPP T-junction. R(W) 0.9m (1.45km), SO(W) road (watch out for wire across track down in dip!), to next road at Upper Chute.

UPPER CHUTE

L(S) 80yds (73m) to T-junction, R(W then S) 0.25m (402m) to crossroads, R(WSW) 200yds (183m), alongside green, to T-junction opposite pub. L(SSW) 0.6m (966m), through R/L dogleg, to T-junction by house at Coldridge Woods. R(SW) through barrier 0.5m (805m) to track crossroads. Bridle-path ahead blocked so R(NW) 150yds (137m) to crossroads, L(SW) 0.25m (402m) to T-junction (easy to shoot through!) then R(NNW) 0.7m (1.13km) to T-junction by gate. SO(NW) 0.9m (1.45km), up Chute Down valley then through woods, to familiar T-junction (you came through the gate opposite earlier). L(SW then S) 0.75m (1.21km), keeping SO(S) on main track, to T-junction. Fork R(S) off main track 0.7m (1.13km) to crossroads then R(NW) 1.5m (2.4km), joining tarmac at 1.2m (1.93km), to The Sheers crossroads. SO(WNW) 0.75m (1.21km) to A338 crossroads, then R(N) 1.25m (2.01km) to start.

COLDRIDGE

SHEERS X-ROADS

Mendip Loop [MAP C]

Distance: 15 miles (24 km)
Time: 2.5 hours (4 hours when wet)
There's precious little off-road round here but this loop takes in some of the best. Watch out for the bare-rock bridleway down to Cheddar – it's like cobbles with skates on when wet!

DOLEBURY BOTTOM

Start at Dolebury Bottom car park (GR446588) off the A38. Go through gate (ESE) 0.25m (402m)

MAP C

TYNING'S FARM

then fork R(S) up side valley 1m (1.6km) then zigzag L/R, over stream, to continue to climb (SE) 1m (1.6km) to Tyning's Farm. Go through yard then turn R(SSW) for 0.2m (322m) on tarmac then keep SO(SSW), when lane turns R(WNW), for 1.6m (2.57km) down technical track (watch out for gate at 1m – 1.62km!) to T-junction. Turn L(E) then almost immediately drop R(SSE) 0.25m (402m) to road. Turn R(W) 0.1m (160m) to T-junction then L(S) then almost immediately L(SE) again for 0.4m (644m), keeping L(E) at next fork, to fork. Here swing R(SSE) and follow lane 0.2m (322m) down to main road at the mouth of

CHEDDAR

Cheddar Gorge (cafe stop if needed and you can cut L up the gorge to rejoin the route on top if it's really wet). Turn L(E) then almost immediately fork R(ESE), keeping L(ESE) immediately after, to

BRADLEY CROSS

climb up to Bradley Cross, to T-junction just after S-bend, 0.6m (966m) away. Turn L then immediately R(ESE) on bridleway in front of house for 0.25m (402m) to gate then keep SO(ESE) 100yds (91m) before swinging L(E), up through gated track and past farm, 0.75m (1.21km) to T-junction. Turn L(ENE) 1.2m (1.93km) to junction

B3135

with B3135. Go SO(ENE) 1m (1.6km) on tarmac to crossroads, turn L(NNW) 1.6m (2.57km), passing through another crossroads, to T-junction then turn L(NNW) 1.1m (1.77km), swinging L(WNW) past mast and going off-road, to boundary. Continue SO(NW) on single-track for

BEACON BATCH

1.1m (1.77km) over Beacon Batch, going past a fork where you keep R(WNW), to bridleway crossroads. Turn R(NNE), downhill, 0.7m (1.13km) to waymarked crossroads then turn L(W) 1.5m (2.4km), joining another track coming from the L at the edge of the woods, down to start.

MAP C

N
E
W
S

Ubley
Compton Wood
Hazel Hill
Cleve Hill
Whitestown Fm
Fernhill Fm
Haydon Grange
Hill Grange
Danger Area
Stow Barrow
Priddy Hill Fm
Chancellor's Fm
Rookery Fm
Hazel Warren Fm
Tumuli
Ubley Drove
MENDIP FOREST
Yoxter Fm
King's Down
Cairn
Tumuli
Cheddar Head
Leaze Fm
Blagdon Hill Fm
Middle Ellick Fm
Ellick Fm
Burlington Ham.
Ubley Warren Fm
Nature Reserve
Paywell Fm
ROMAN FORT
Manor Fm
Charterhouse
Vater Bottom
Warren Bottom
Earthwork
Long Wood
Wellington Fm
Tumulus
Beacon Batch ☆325
Black Down
Goatchurch Cavern
Burrington Combe
Nature Reserve
Mendip Lodge Wood
Dolebury Warren
Rowberrow Warren
Warren Hq
Tyning's Fm
Cave
Gorse Bigbury Grange
West Mendip Way
Piney Sleight
Piney Sleight Fm
Black Rock
Cheddar Cliffs
Cheddar Gorge
Totty Pot Cave
Carscliff Fm
Bradley Cross
Cheddar
West Mendip Way
Longbottom
Ashridge Fm
Tumuli
The Perch
Hythe
Shipham
Cock Hill
Cheddar Wood
Cheddar Reservoir
Sewage Wks
Winterhead
Winterhead Hill
Gallow
Quarry Fm
Fry's Hill
St Michael's Cheshire Home
Nyland Manor
Halfway House
Star
Sidcot
Oakridge
Hale Coombe
Shute Shelve Hill
Rose
Winscombe
Sandford Batch
Thimbleston Batch
Paddington Ho
Bourton Fm
Cross Plain
King's Wood
Hospl
Axbridge
Cross
Weare
Shute
Sparrow
Brinscombe
Cradle Br
Cheddar Yeo

APPENDICES

The following pages are a directory of useful contacts for the Wessex Way off-road cyclist including YHAs, bike shops, National Trust, Local Authority and Association offices.

Weather News
Sussex
☎ 0891 500 402
Hampshire
☎ 0891 500 403
Somerset/Wilts
☎ 0891 500 405

Tourist Information Centres
Weston-super-Mare
☎ 0934 626838
Cheddar
☎ 0934 744071
Wells
☎ 0749 672552
Warminster
☎ 0985 218548
Marlborough
☎ 0672 513989
Newbury
☎ 0635 30267
Winchester
☎ 0962 840500
Petersfield
☎ 0730 268829
Arundel
☎ 0903 882268/ 882419
Brighton
☎ 0273 323755
Eastbourne
☎ 0323 411400

Youth Hostels
YHA, Trevelyan House, 8 St Stephen's Hill, St Albans, Herts AL1 2DY. ☎ 0727 855215
YHA South England Region, 11b York Road, Salisbury, Wilts. ☎ 0722 337515
Youth Hostels en-route
Cheddar, Somerset
☎ 0934 742494
Truleigh Hill, W Sussex
☎ 0903 813419
Telscombe, E Sussex
☎ 0273 301357
Alfriston, E Sussex
☎ 0323 870423
Eastbourne,E Sussex
☎ 0323 721081

Camping (South Downs)
Write to: Sussex Downs Conservation Project County Planning Dept, County Hall, Chichester, W Sussex PO19 1RL. ☎ 0243 777618

Bike Shops
These are just a selection of the many bike shops that are accessible to Wessex Way riders:
AVON
Les Wilkins (Cycles) Ltd, 10 Walliscote Road, Weston-Super-Mare, Avon. ☎ 0934 629370
SOMERSET
Cheddar Bicycle Centre Ltd, Tweentown, Cheddar, Somerset. ☎ 0934 742955.
Bikes Bits, 49 Cuthbert Street, Wells, Somerset. ☎ 0749 670260
WILTSHIRE
Batchelors (Cycles) 72, Market Place, Warminster, Wiltshire. ☎ 0985 213221
Elite Cycles Unit 1, Bourne Works, Collingbourne Ducis, Wiltshire. ☎ 0264 85086
HAMPSHIRE
Peter Hargrove Cycles, 26 Jewry Street, Winchester, Hampshire. ☎ 0962 860005
Mountain Bike Warehouse (MTB Hire), Queen Elizabeth

Country Park, Hampshire. ☎ 0585 322849
The Sensible Bicycle Company, Station Road, Liss, nr Petersfield, Hampshire.
☎ 0730 894884

SUSSEX (EAST & WEST)
The Storrington Cyclist, The Forge, 38 West Street, Storrington, Sussex. ☎ 0903 745534
Arun Bicycles, 30b Southgate, Chichester, Sussex. ☎ 0243 537337
Arun Bicycles, 50 The Street, Rustington, Sussex. ☎ 0903 850418
The Mountain Bike Centre, 46/56 Portland Road, Worthing, Sussex.
☎ 0903 234445
Mud, Sweat Gears, 20 Crabtree Lane, Lancing, Sussex. ☎ 0903 752308
Cyclomania Cycle Centre, 24 Boundary Road, Hove, Sussex.
☎ 0273 420950
Nevada Bikes, 1 Green Street, Eastbourne, Sussex. ☎ 0323 411549

British Rail Booking Information
Bristol
☎ 0272 294255
Brighton
☎ 0273 206755
Reading
☎ 0734 595911

National Trust
Wessex Regional Offices, Eastleigh Court, Bishopstrow, Warminster, Wiltshire.
☎ 0985 847777
Southern Regional Offices, Polesden Lacey, Dorking, Surrey.
☎ 0372 53401
East Sussex Regional Offices, Scotney Castle, Lamberhurst, Tunbridge Wells, Kent.
☎ 0892 890651

County Council Offices (Rights of Way)
If you meet an access problem along the Way – whether it's a missing waymarker, locked gates, excess overgrowth, an impassable quagmire or other obstruction – then do report it to the relevant Rights of Way department. They will take steps to sort it out.
Avon
☎ 0272 226531
Somerset
☎ 0823 333451
Wiltshire
☎ 0225 713000
Berkshire
☎ 0734 234234
Hampshire
☎ 0962 841841
West Sussex
☎ 0243 777618

East Sussex
☎ 0273 477851

The Cyclists Touring Club
Since 1878 the Cyclists Touring Club (CTC) has been the governing body for recreational cycling in this country. It currently has 40000 members, 200 nationwide clubs and 100 local clubs affiliated to it.

Recently the CTC has taken on responsibility for addressing off-road cycling access issues and representing the views of mountain bikers at a local and national level. If you would like to apply for membership then please apply to:
CTC, Dept CSB/94, 69 Meadrow, Godalming, Surrey GU7 3HS.
☎ **0483 417217.**

Benefits of being a member include: representation on Rights of Way and access issues in your area. 3rd Party insurance cover. Free legal advice for cycling related problems. Free legal aid. Free technical advice. Free international touring info. Bi-monthly colour magazine. Free handbook. Mail order service. A voice in MTB.